LEARN TO SCUBA DIVE IN A WEEKEND

LEARN TO
SCUBA DIVE
IN A WEEKEND

REG VALLINTINE

Photography by Brian Pitkin

ALFRED A. KNOPF
New York
1993

A DORLING KINDERSLEY BOOK

This edition is a Borzoi Book published in 1993 by Alfred A. Knopf, Inc., by arrangement with Dorling Kindersley.

Designer Emma Boys
Editor Sarah Larter
Series Art Editor Amanda Lunn
Series Editor Jo Weeks
Managing Editor Sean Moore
Managing Art Editor Tina Vaughan
Production Controller Helen Creeke

Library of Congress Cataloging-in-Publication Data
Vallintine, Reg.
Learn scuba diving in a weekend / by Reg Vallintine. --1st ed.
p.   cm. -- (Learn in a weekend series)
Includes index.

ISBN 0-679-342228-5
1. Scuba diving. I. Title. II. Series
GV840.S78V34 1993
797.2'3--dc20   92-54794
CIP
Computer page make-up by
Cloud 9 Designs
Reproduced by Colourscan,
Singapore
Printed and bound by
Arnoldo Mondadori,
Verona, Italy
First American ed.

CONTENTS

·

Introduction 6

PREPARING FOR THE WEEKEND 8

What to wear 10
Essential equipment 12
Scuba structure..................14
Science & diving.................16
Fit to dive............................18
First aid 20
The diver's language 22

THE WEEKEND COURSE 24

Day 1

Snorkeling 26
Suiting up............................30
Entering & submerging 32
Ability & mobility...............36
Buoyancy control 42
Ditch & retrieve...................46
Recovery..............................50

Day 2

Decompression 52
Prevention & cure 54
Shoreline diving..................58
Boat diving 62
Using a marker buoy............70

AFTER THE WEEKEND 72

Scuba sense 74
Care & equipment...............76
Advancing............................78
What next?...........................80
Diverse dives........................82
Conservation 84
Friend or foe?.......................86
Oceans of adventure............88

Glossary 92
Index 94
Getting in touch 96
Acknowledgments 96

INTRODUCTION

TO LEARN TO **SCUBA** DIVE in a weekend may appear to be
an impossible task, especially to all those ancient divers
who have spent so many years building up their ability and
technique. However, times have changed, and we now
know that providing someone can swim, is moderately fit,
and, above all, eager to learn, the basics of the sport can be
taught in two days. To gain full enjoyment, and also to
prevent exhaustion, you may decide that it is better
to split your training into several longer sessions
over a few weeks. Remember that short courses
and first sea dives must always be taken with
a qualified instructor, who will be concerned
with building your skill and enhancing your
enjoyment, not their own. If you take
things at your own speed, in no time
you will find you will be able to drift

along tropical coral reefs, explore historical wrecks, or even enjoy the unique challenges of cooler waters. Your equipment is reliable and foolproof, nevertheless, scuba diving does take place in an unpredictable environment. Before you receive a certificate of competence you must learn the theoretical aspects in greater detail, so that you can avoid the problems associated with the sport, and know how to cope should they arise. The rewards of learning this sport will be worthwhile, and practicing the exercises presented in this book will make you feel more confident in your use of **scuba**.

REG VALLINTINE

PREPARING FOR THE WEEKEND

*Practical preparation for your **scuba** diving weekend*

•

THE AMOUNT OF ENJOYMENT AND SATISFACTION that you will gain from **scuba** diving depends on the amount of preparation you make before you even enter the water. Before you start to dive, be sure that you do not have a physical condition that would make the activity dangerous for you. You must sign a medical declaration, and also pass an examination with a doctor (see pp.18-19). It is also very important to make sure that you are at ease in water. If you are a weak swimmer, then get lots of practice because, although you will not have to prove you can swim fast or far, you will be asked to demonstrate that you can swim. A sound

Fins

Wetsuit

COMMUNICATION
Underwater you must use a system of recognized hand signals to exchange important messages with your fellow divers. Memorize all of the signals (see pp.22-23) before you even enter the water.

CLOTHING
Make certain that you know precisely what items of clothing and gear you will require before you embark on your **scuba** diving course. Good, well-fitting equipment is essential for trouble-free diving (see pp.10-13). Your instructor or school will probably provide it initially.

SMB

comprehension of how each part of your breathing equipment functions is important so that you trust and have confidence in it prior to breathing underwater. One of the most important decisions that you make will be where, and with whom you will learn to dive. If you intend to learn to dive in a resort, you may choose to do your preliminary training locally, with a recognized school or club, this way you can more quickly enjoy the underwater sights abroad. Wherever you choose to learn though, it is crucial that you are under the supervision of a fully qualified instructor. Never risk taking tuition from someone with whom you cannot communicate or who has an unrecognized teaching certificate. You must also make sure that you establish the signals you are going to use underwater before you leave dry land and avoid later problems.

BC

*As you read this book, you will notice that some words are in **bold**, these are defined in the glossary (see pp.92-93).*

Gauges

EQUIPMENT
Diving requires specialized equipment such as the **BC**, to aid and control **buoyancy**. Your gauges and watch are vital pieces of equipment, acting as guides to the depth and time of your dives (see pp.12-13).

SAFETY AND SCIENCE
Scuba diving requires a certain elementary understanding of science. Even as a learner diver you must know the effects that changes in pressure have on the body when you travel underwater. You must comprehend the need to ascend slowly to prevent **DCS** and **burst lung**, and know how to go through the vital process of **ear clearing** (see pp.18-21).

WHAT TO WEAR

Essential clothing and gear for the diver

EVERY SPORT HAS specialized equipment and clothing that must be used, and **scuba** diving is no exception. Make sure you know what equipment you will need before you begin your diving course; while some diving schools will supply all the necessary equipment apart from your swimming costume and towel, others may expect you to have your own basic equipment of mask, fins, and snorkel. If you are learning in open or cool water, you may also need a lightweight **neoprene** wetsuit or jacket to keep you warm – you should also check beforehand whether these will be supplied.

Tube　　　*Rubber mouthpiece*

SNORKELS •
The snorkel is a simple tube with an attached mouthpiece. When you swim on the surface it allows you to breathe without raising your head.

• MASKS
Diving masks cover your eyes and nose, enabling you to see clearly underwater. They are made of ordinary or translucent silicone rubber. As they come in various shapes and sizes, they should be fitted properly, so there is no possibility that they will leak underwater.

• FINS
Fins allow you to glide effortlessly through the water, using a slow crawl kick and leaving your hands and arms free. Those that are used for initial training and pool use have a comfortable full support for your foot; those that are used for open water are larger and stiffer, with an adjustable strap: this allows them to be worn over your boots.

THE BASICS

Take care that all your equipment fits properly before you enter the water; make sure it is comfortable and easy to wear. You will discover that masks, fins, and snorkels come in various guises, so try on several types until you are satisfied. Avoid any problems by taking advice from a reputable dive shop, or your instructor.

• GLOVES
For very cold water, you will find that a pair of protective **neoprene** gloves are a good idea. In warmer water they will also protect your hands from any bites, scrapes, scratches, and stings.

• BOOTS
Neoprene boots are a standard addition to the wetsuit, and they are a necessity when you are using adjustable fins, keeping your feet warm and covered. Most boots have hard rubber soles that protect your feet from injury when you are entering the water over stones and rocks.

WETSUITS

Although the water will be warm if you are learning in a pool or tropical sea, you will still get cold as the body loses heat 25 times more quickly in water than in air. Wetsuits come in varying thicknesses, so ensure you choose one to suit the temperature of the water in which you dive.

• ZIP
Suits have zips for easy fitting.

• HOOD
A hood attached to the jacket or suit covers your head and keeps it warm.

• BODY
All suits will protect your body from minor scratches, cuts, and stings in the water.

• ALL-IN-ONE
Some divers prefer to use an all-in-one suit, which covers the body, providing complete insulation from head to toe.

• LONG JOHN
Wetsuits for colder water have a long john consisting of trousers attached to a vest that can be worn with a jacket.

NEOPRENE SUITS

Protection against the cold depends on the thickness of the **neoprene** that wetsuits are made of. In warm or tropical water 3-5mm ($1/8$-$1/5$in) is adequate. For colder water, suits can be 6-8mm ($1/4$-$1/3$ in) thick. Wetsuits trap a layer of water between you and the **neoprene**, which heats up to aid insulation. Dry suits are sealed at the cuffs, letting in no water at all. An undersuit known as a "woolly bear" keeps the diver warm in cold conditions.

Neoprene Wetsuit

Water • • Skin
• Neoprene

Neoprene Dry suit

Water • • Skin
• Air
• Neoprene

ESSENTIAL EQUIPMENT

Equipment to be aware of and understand before diving

IN ADDITION to the basic equipment, there are other specialized items a novice diver needs to recognize and know how to use, to ensure the safety of themselves and others, and to ease progression when underwater. Some, such as gauges and the compass, are initially used by your instructor, but you should understand their function because you will learn to use them with experience. The **buoyancy compensator (BC)** should be worn by all who dive and its functions must be thoroughly understood.

BARE NECESSITIES

Diving equipment is designed to be safe and compact. Quick-releases are a typical feature of buckles and straps, allowing you to ditch your equipment rapidly, and with the minimum of fuss. Knives, flashlights, and gauges can all be strapped to your limbs, so that they do not protrude dangerously.

Weight

• WEIGHT BELTS
The belt should have a quick-release catch so that you can drop it if necessary. Weights thread on to the belt and come in various sizes. You should carry enough to allow you to sink effortlessly.

• FLASHLIGHT
Underwater flashlights are essential for night dives. They also allow you to see into caves and wrecks, illuminate marine life, and see colors that otherwise filter out at depth (see p.17).

Pocket flashlight

Standard flashlight

Cutting edge

Sheath

• KNIVES
It may be useful – and occasionally vital – to have a knife. It should have a serrated cutting edge and a rubber sheath to attach it to your calf.

CONSOLE •
Your gauges and compass can be worn strapped to one arm, or alternatively on a console that connects to your breathing apparatus.

• WATCH
The simplest method of assessing the length of your dive is to use a diving watch with an adjustable **bezel** that indicates when you left the surface.

• DEPTH GAUGE
Depth gauges register your depth, either with a simple needle reading or digitally. The more expensive models can also tell you how long you have been underwater.

• COMPASS
Using a compass is part of your more advanced training (see p.79). It gives you greater awareness of your position underwater.

BUOYANCY

The **buoyancy compensator (BC)** is an indispensable piece of diving equipment. It fastens around your chest and stomach, and connects to your breathing apparatus. It allows you to vary your **buoyancy** when you are underwater, control your ascents safely, and support yourself at the surface.

SUPPORT HANDLE •
The support handle on the back of the jacket is useful for lifting your **BC** when the cumbersome **scuba** tank is connected to it. Once you enter the water, the whole thing becomes virtually weightless.

AIR OUT •
A **dump valve** is located on the right shoulder. It allows you to expel air rapidly from your **BC** to control an ascent if you need to do so (see p.44).

• HOSE
This corrugated tube is held above your head when you expel air from your jacket.

• HARNESS
The **BC** attaches you to your breathing apparatus with a harness that straps securely around the tank, fastening with a clamp.

WAIST STRAPS •
Your **BC** secures firmly around your body with adjustable straps. that are easy to undo, should you need to ditch your equipment.

• AIR CONTROLS
The round control allows you to inflate the **BC** with air from a **direct feed** that runs from your **regulator**. The square control allows you to deflate the BC.

MOUTHPIECE •
The mouthpiece allows you to inflate your **BC** for support at the surface (see p.51).

SURFACE MARKERS

If you are likely to be diving in a current or drift diving, it will be necessary for you to use a **surface marker buoy (SMB)**. This is connected to a reel of line, which is held by one member of the dive team, and unwound during the course of your dive. Buoys are usually inflated at surface and are left there, as you descend to the sea bed. Clearly visible to boats, they indicate your exact position underwater.

Reel

While submerged, your cover boat should fly the International Code of Signals **A-flag**. This has as its second meaning: "I have a diver down: keep clear and at slow speed". It is a distinctive blue and white flag, and should also be flown on a mast above the surface marker buoy. In America, a red flag with a white diagonal line across it is sometimes used, but it is not recognized officially.

A-flag

Buoy

SUB

Buoy

SCUBA STRUCTURE

The components of your underwater breathing equipment

THE SCUBA, or self-contained underwater breathing apparatus, is the most vital piece of equipment for the diver. It allows you to breathe underwater with ease and stay submerged for a limited period of time to explore the marine world. The scuba consists of a tank of **compressed air** and a **regulator** or demand valve, which adjusts the pressure of the air and includes the mouthpiece. It attaches to your **BC** by means of a metal clamp.

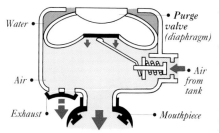

- *Water*
- *Purge valve (diaphragm)*
- *Air*
- *Air from tank*
- *Exhaust*
- *Mouthpiece*

MOUTHPIECE

As you breathe in, pressure drops in the **demand valve**, and the diaphragm is pushed towards the mouth by the external water pressure. This triggers a lever that allows air in. Each mouthful of air is fed at the same pressure as the surrounding water.

THE REGULATOR

The **regulator first-stage** fits onto a **pillar valve** with an **A-clamp**. The first-stage reduces the air pressure to about 10 **bar** (145lb/in^2), above that of the surrounding water pressure. The air then travels down a tube to the regulator **second-stage**, which includes your breathing mouthpiece. Inside the second-stage is the **purge valve**. This is in contact with water on one side and has an air space on the other, which refills as you breathe.

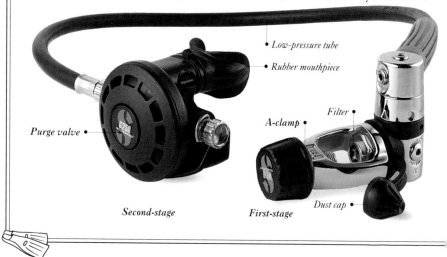

- *Low-pressure tube*
- *Rubber mouthpiece*
- *Filter*
- *A-clamp*
- *Purge valve*
- *Dust cap*

Second-stage   *First-stage*

THE AIR TANK

A **scuba** tank can be manufactured from either steel or aluminum, and is made to withstand the very high pressures of the air inside – usually 200 **bar** (3000lb/in^2). Particulars of this, along with working pressure, test pressure, and the tank's specifications are imprinted onto its exterior. It is filled from a compressor that takes air from the atmosphere, compresses it, and pumps it into the tank. When not in use, tanks are stored in a cool place, with a little **compressed air** in them, switched off and on their sides.

SWITCHING ON

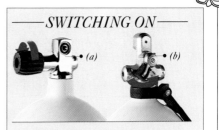

(a)   *(b)*

The **pillar valve** in the neck of the tank allows it to be filled with air, and includes the **O-ring** seal. A tap opens and closes the tank. Two types of tap exist: (*a*) works in the same way as a household tap, turning it fully counter-clockwise to switch on. To switch on type (*b*), you push the lever out and over to the side. Make sure you know which way to turn.

First-stage

Pillar valve

Handle

Protective mesh

Second-stage

• OCTOPUS RIG
The **octopus rig** connects directly to the tank; it must be easily distinguishable from the primary mouthpiece and air tube. It is used to give another diver air in a situation where they have run out.

• PRESSURE TUBE
A high-pressure tube connects the **regulator first-stage** to the contents gauge, which registers air pressure. When the needle reaches 50 **bar** (725lb/in^2) you must surface.

• DIRECT FEED
The **direct feed** tube connects up to your **BC** (see p.13), so that you can inflate your jacket with **compressed air** from your tank to increase **buoyancy**.

• TANK BOOT
The tank boot, usually made of rubber, fits onto the bottom of it to enable it to stand upright and protect it from any bumps or knocks.

• PURGE VALVE
Depressing the **purge valve** pushes air through to the mouthpiece. The purge button also rids the **second-stage** of any drops of water that may have entered it.

SCIENCE & DIVING

The laws of physics and the underwater world

•

WHEN YOU DIVE, you enter another aspect of the natural world that is governed by a different set of physical laws. At sea level, air pressure is equal to a force of approximately 1 **bar**, or 14$\frac{1}{2}$lb/in². To change this pressure significantly on land, you would have to travel higher than the summit of Mount Everest at 8,848m (29,000ft). The air pressure would then have changed from 1 bar (14$\frac{1}{2}$lb/in²) at **atmospheric pressure**, to virtually zero. Changes in pressure underwater are far more dramatic. For every 10m (33ft), that you descend, pressure increases by 1 bar (14$\frac{1}{2}$lb/in²), and volume of air decreases. This pressure is lost by the same amount as you ascend.

LAWS OF PRESSURE

A glass turned upside down and held on the water's surface will trap air at a pressure of approximately 1 bar (14$\frac{1}{2}$lb/in²). Pushed through the water, rim first, to 10m (33ft) the air is forced into half the space, and pressure doubles. Pressure triples, and the air occupies a third of the space at 20m (66ft), while at 30m (100ft), the air pressure quadruples, and the air space is quartered. Pressure alters at a fixed rate, but the greatest changes in volume will occur closer to the surface.

0.24 bar

Changes to air pressure at height

Atmospheric pressure at sea level

1 bar

full

2 bar

½ volume

3 bar

⅓ volume

4 bar

¼ volume

10,000m (33,000ft)

Not to scale

Sea level

10m (33ft)

20m (66ft)

30m (100ft)

Below sea level

THE AIR WE BREATHE

The air that you breathe is composed mainly of oxygen (O_2) and nitrogen (N_2), with a tiny proportion of other gases. The space that these gases occupy reduces with the increased pressure as you descend; the reverse happens on ascent. Therefore, you must understand the effect that this will have on the body's air spaces, such as the ears and lungs (see p.19), and take measures to prevent injury.

O_2 approx. 21%.
This gas is essential
for you to live

Others approx. 1%

N_2 approx. 78%.
Most of the air we
breathe is nitrogen,
which can cause severe
problems for divers
(see pp.52-53, 56-57)

ASCENDING
If you ascend after a dive, holding your breath, the volume of air inside your lungs will expand. Ascending too quickly can cause serious injury such as **burst lung**.

LIGHT & COLOR

As you dive to greater depths, light will be absorbed, and colors lose their natural vibrancy. The first color that disappears from the spectrum is red. Other colors follow, and the only way you can recapture their original hue is to use the artificial light of a flashlight or a camera flash.

The most exciting sea life is found in shallow water. As you go deeper the scenery is less colorful, and there is little to be seen.

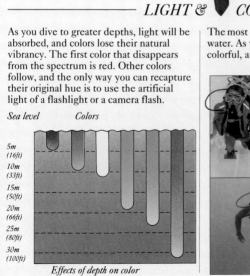

Sea level   *Colors*

5m
(16ft)
10m
(33ft)
15m
(50ft)
20m
(66ft)
25m
(80ft)
30m
(100ft)

Effects of depth on color

Left: Shallow water allows in more light and consequently you can see more color

Below: At greater depths, the reduced light means that less color can be seen

A FIT DIVER

*Health matters to understand before you learn to **scuba** dive*

WHEN TAKING UP DIVING, as with any sport, you should be healthy and fairly fit before you begin your instruction. It is not a dangerous sport if you are careful, take note of what your instructor teaches you, and follow the rules. You may have heard of specific diving diseases, such as **nitrogen narcosis** and **decompression sickness**, sometimes referred to as "the bends". However these dangers are easily avoided provided you take the proper precautions. Before you start training, complete a medical declaration. This should be approved by your doctor before you go into the open water. Age limits vary between organizations, but most would not recommend **scuba** training for those younger than 13, and there is no upper age limit if you are fit – some people have taken up the sport in their seventies.

AQUA-ABILITY

Before you learn to dive you need to be a reasonably competent swimmer. Although using a **BC** will give you the ability to control your **buoyancy** and float easily on the surface, you will not normally have enough confidence to enjoy **scuba** diving unless you feel naturally at home in water.

It is important to be relaxed enough under the water to make brief dives from the surface, holding your breath. When your diving course starts, you will probably be asked to swim for a distance of about 20m (66ft), to attest to your ability. This is not a test of speed or strength, so don't rush it.

AIR IN THE BODY

Owing to increases in pressure under the water, pockets of air in your body are affected by diving. The main air cavities are your lungs. There are also pockets of air in your stomach. These will not be affected though, unless you have inadvertently swallowed air. Ears are also affected by pressure; to rid yourself of the discomfort caused by this, you must learn a vital process called **ear clearing** (see p.33).

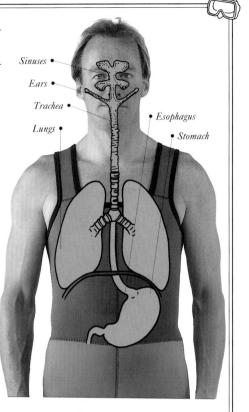

Sinuses •
Ears •
Trachea •
Lungs •
• Esophagus
• Stomach

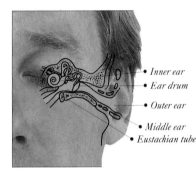

• Inner ear
• Ear drum
• Outer ear
• Middle ear
• Eustachian tube

YOUR EAR
Your ear consists of the outer, inner, and middle ear. Your outer and middle ear are divided by a membrane called the eardrum, while the eustachian tube connects the middle ear to the area at the back of your nose and throat. The inner ear, above this, contains your organs of hearing and balance.

LUNGS AND STOMACH
The primary air spaces in your body are your lungs. As you breathe into them from your **regulator**, the air pressure in them adjusts to that of the surrounding water, so they do not squeeze. If you trap air in the stomach it distends as you rise, expanding with the lessening pressure. A burp clears extra air.

MEDICAL CHECKLIST

• It is vital that you check with your doctor and have a good medical examination prior to starting to dive. This is particularly so if you have a history of diabetes, high blood pressure, epilepsy, blackouts, heart or lung disorders, or dependency on drugs.
• If you are in doubt about your suitability, ask your instructor for a medical form and get your doctor to examine you anyway. If he feels that it would be useful to have the opinion of a diving doctor, your instructor will be able to suggest who is suitable.
• If you are unlucky enough to burst an eardrum, it will usually heal rapidly, but

always have a medical check before diving again. This also applies if you have any doubts about the condition of your ears. You must not dive with a heavy cold as the mucus may have blocked your eustachian tube and sinuses, thus making the process of **ear clearing** more difficult. If you have any temporary conditions that affect your nose, sinuses, or lungs, it is better not to start diving until they have cleared up.
• Do not dive if you are taking any drugs or medication that may make you drowsy.
• Women who are pregnant are advised not to take up diving during this period.

First Aid

What you need to know in case a medical emergency occurs

Although diving is not a dangerous sport, divers do operate in an alien environment. If you lose consciousness underwater you can die unless help is at hand. This is why the first rule for divers is: "never dive alone". Dangers from the local inhabitants are generally exaggerated, but you need to know how to deal with cuts, scratches, and stings, which can heal more slowly than on land. It is very important, too, that you know how to resuscitate a diver who has stopped breathing. Most dive centers, schools, and boats will have the necessary kit and equipment, including pure oxygen for serious diving complaints, but you should be able to deal with minor diving ailments. It is worth taking a first aid course.

A Kit for Divers

In addition to a standard first aid kit, there are some specific remedies for stings and scratches that are peculiar to marine life. Speak to a diving doctor for advice on suitable brands. Take an emergency handbook on trips so that you know how to deal with particular diving emergencies.

——IDEAL EXTRAS——

An ideal first aid kit should include:
• Pure oxygen – for rapid treatment of **decompression sickness**, etc.
• Fluids – for decompression sickness.
• Vinegar – for treating jellyfish stings.
• Pain relievers and decongestants.
• Elastic, pressure, and crêpe bandages.
• Gauze swabs.
• Assorted band-aids.
• Scissors, tweezers, sharp knife, needle.
• Blankets, hot-water bottles.
• Head packs, cold packs.
• Pen and paper, coins or tokens for use in public telephones, and a flashlight.

Decongestant pills – to clear the sinuses

Sea sickness pills

Anti-histamine pills – for relief from stings

Mouthpiece attachment

Eye wash – to remove foreign bodies from eyes and relieve redness

Mouthpiece for resuscitation

Iodine – for coral cuts and grazes

Eye bath

Cotton wool

Ear drops – to loosen ear wax

Magnesium sulphate for removal of sea urchin spines

RESUSCITATION

If a serious accident does happen and there is any delay in recovery from the water, the victim may stop breathing. Check the victim's chest, nose, and mouth for signs of respiration. If breathing has stopped, the victim's skin will be bluish-white, especially around the lips, ear lobes, and fingernails. On land, **artificial respiration**, as shown here, must commence. Artificial respiration in water is covered on pp.50-51.

1. CLEAR AIRWAY
Lie the victim on their back lifting the head so that the neck is extended and their airway is clear and open.

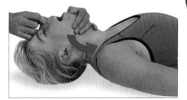

2. SHUT AND OPEN
Hold the victim's nose shut, seal your mouth to their lips, and blow four quick breaths into them to inflate their lungs.

3. LOOK AND BREATHE
Continue to breathe at a rhythm of 20-30 breaths per minute. Turn your head in between each breath to check for movement in the chest.

RECOVERY POSITION

COMFORT
Ensure the head is supported and that the airway is not obstructed.

When practicing resuscitation, continue to breathe for the victim until medical help arrives, or the victim starts to breathe and color returns to their face, or you are unable to continue. When their breathing restarts, put them in the recovery position.

• **ARMS**
Bring the upper arm over the body, ensuring the lower arm is tucked in.

• **CHEST**
The chest should be comfortable, so that the patient can breathe easily.

• **LEGS**
The upper leg is forward to balance the body. The lower leg is extended.

THE DIVER'S LANGUAGE

*The essential method of communication for all **scuba** divers*

AS YOU SINK BELOW the surface, the noises of the normal world disappear, replaced by the hiss and bubble of your underwater breathing. As the underwater environment prevents normal conversation, it is crucial that you are able to communicate by some other means when you dive. The method used is a system of internationally recognized hand signals, and it is essential you learn them thoroughly. They should be made clearly and firmly to your fellow divers, so that there is no chance of any misunderstanding.

THE HAND SIGNALS

There are basically nine underwater hand signals. These can be grouped logically into three groups of three. The first three concern wellbeing, the second your air supply, and the last, direction. There are also two surface signals that must be learned.

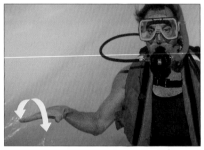

NOT OK?/SOMETHING WRONG
If you have a problem for any reason, hold your hand flat, and tilt it from side-to-side.

"ARE YOU OK?"/"I AM OK"
The first, most frequently used signal, must be practiced from the start of your lessons. It must always be responded to instantly.

"I NEED IMMEDIATE HELP!"
An emergency signal made by waving your forearm to and fro with your fist clenched – it should be followed by instant assistance.

"I HAVE NO AIR!"
An emergency signal, this indicates a need for air.

ON RESERVE
This indicates your contents gauge shows a low pressure.

OUT OF BREATH
Use this signal to indicate you are tired and need to recover.

• NOT OK
A waved arm at the surface means "we need help now". As with its underwater counterpart, it is an emergency signal that should result in rapid help from a boat or the shore.

• OK
This indicates to your boat or shore party that you are OK at the surface.

THUMBS UP
A thumb up ends a dive, down starts it.

DIRECTION
Your index finger can indicate a particular direction, or is used to point towards you, or to a fellow diver.

STOP!
To halt another diver for any reason, put your hand with the palm outward and in a vertical position.

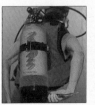

OTHER SIGNALS

In addition to the hand signals, there are other recognized signals that you need to be aware of before you go underwater.
• Sound travels more quickly in water than air. If your co-divers cannot see you, but you need help, attract attention by banging your tank with your knife. This results in them turning to look. You can then give the normal "I need help" hand signal.
• On a night dive, you need to be able to signal with your flashlight underwater and on surface. Signals can be created by moving the flashlight. For example, you could move the beam in circles to signify OK, or from side-to-side to mean help.

NOISE
Bang your tank with your knife to create a distinctive noise, and attract attention.

LIGHT
On a night or a cave dive, it is vital that you take a flashlight (see pp.82-83).

THE WEEKEND COURSE

The fundamentals of your two day **scuba** *diving course*

THE COURSE covers twelve basic **scuba** diving skills, set over a period of two days and amounting to a minimum of twelve hours. The first day's skills are set in safe, calm water, such as a swimming pool. These initial hours will build your confidence and ability, and familiarize you with every piece of equipment. Day two takes you through elementary theory, which must be learned in detail before you qualify as a diver, and then into the exciting new world of open water. Follow the course under the guidance of a good instructor, don't rush it, and above all try to enjoy yourself.

Safe at surface

DAY 1		Hours	Page
SKILL 1	Snorkeling	$1/2$	26-29
SKILL 2	Suiting up	$1/4$	30-31
SKILL 3	Entering & submerging	$1\frac{1}{4}$	32-35
SKILL 4	Ability & mobility	1	36-41
SKILL 5	Buoyancy control	$1\frac{1}{2}$	42-45
SKILL 6	Ditch & retrieve	$3/4$	46-49
SKILL 7	Recovery	$3/4$	50-51

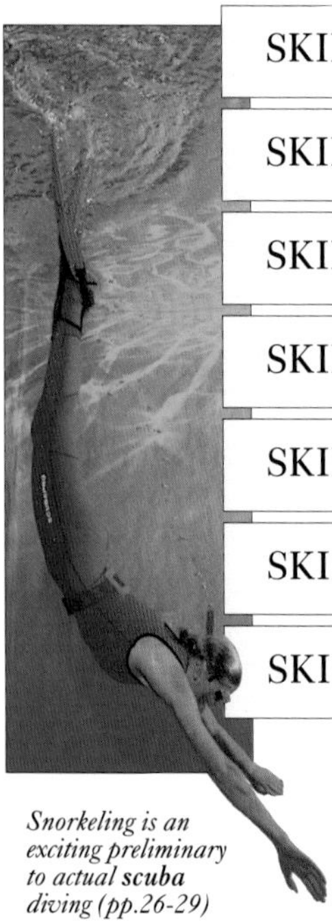

Snorkeling is an exciting preliminary to actual **scuba** *diving (pp.26-29)*

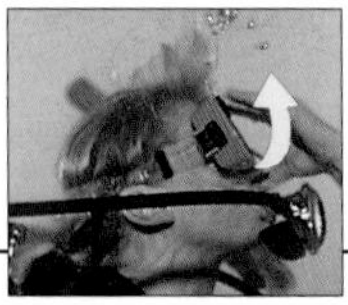

Mask clearing (p.34)

Going down (pp.36-37)

KEY TO SYMBOLS

CLOCKS
All skills are accompanied by clocks. Approximate times for each are shown by the blue section. Time spent on previous skills are colored grey.

ARROWS
The step-by-step pictures are enhanced by the artwork arrows to indicate the direction *under water* that your body should move or be pointing. Yellow arrows

have been used for underwater pictures. Above the surface the arrows used are colored pink.

above water

••• RATING SYSTEM
Every skill is given a rating. Signified with dots, one (•) denotes that the exercise will have a low level of complexity. Five dots (•••••) indicate that you may find the skill less straightforward, and more challenging, and thus need more time to accomplish it.

Rolling backward (p.62)

Small boat entry (p.62)

DAY 2	Hours	Page
SKILL 8 Decompression	1	52-53
SKILL 9 Prevention & cure	1	54-57
SKILL 10 Shoreline diving	1	58-61
SKILL 11 Boat diving	2$^{1}/_{2}$	62-67
SKILL 12 Using a marker buoy	$^{1}/_{2}$	70-71

Time to come up (p.67).

Taking the open water plunge (p.63)

*A **surface marker buoy** informs a cover boat of your exact position underwater (pp.70-71)*

SNORKELING

DAY 1

Definition: *Fitting and using your basic equipment*

SNORKELING IS A SPORT in its own right, using the basic equipment of mask, fins, and snorkel, and provides an excellent basis from which to learn **scuba** diving. If you have never used fins before, it is best to start with these alone and when you are familiar with them, add the rest of the basics. Thrilling and enjoyable, this pastime is easily mastered, and once you have gained confidence in the activity, you will be able to swim face down on the surface of the water and view the undersea world, breathing all the time.

OBJECTIVE: Confidence with the basics. *Rating* ••

GETTING STARTED

Fitting your equipment and starting to snorkel

——— Step 1 ———
FITTING EQUIPMENT

Press the mask against your face without fitting the strap, breathe in through your nose and look down; a well-fitting mask will stick to your face. The snorkel attaches to the side.

WETSUIT •
In a pool you will still feel the cold; a lightweight suit counteracts this.

BUOYANCY •
Wetsuits increase your **buoyancy**, so you may need to add a weight belt.

FINS •
You may find it easier to fit your fins once you are in the water as you will find it proves difficult to walk in them.

MASK AND SNORKEL
Put your mask on your face, pulling the strap over your head, with the snorkel in place. Bite on the two lugs on the mouthpiece. The guard fits between your lips and gums.

Step 2
BREATHING

Standing in the shallows, lean forward from the waist and lower your face into the water, looking down. Get used to breathing through the tube in this position. Ensure that your snorkel is upright. Practice snorkel clearing.

• EASY CLEARING

Clearing your snorkel is one of the first things you will learn.

BREATHE EASY

You may find that breathing through the snorkel is not as easy as it appears, or you may get the hang of it quickly. Breathe through your mouth in a relaxed manner.

CLEARING THE SNORKEL

If water splashes into the snorkel, try to blow it out again with sharp puffs of air from your mouth. This may take practice, but it is an essential part of breathing procedure.

Step 3
STARTING TO SNORKEL

LEG POSITION •

Avoid bending at the knees or using a bicycling action. Attempt to keep your legs reasonably straight. When you are confident, you can even try finning in an upright position.

• BEAT THE FEET

Beat your fins up and down in a slow and rhythmic crawl-style kick. Try to avoid splashing with them, positioning yourself so they are always below the surface.

When you feel ready, start finning slowly across the surface of the water watching the bottom. Build up your experience until you feel confident snorkeling in deeper water. With this simple technique, you will be able to see so much of the underwater world.

JUMPING & DIVING

Jumping in and making your first surface dive

MASK •
Holding the mask will prevent it being lost as you hit the water. Don't look down or the faceplate of your mask will hit the water first.

WEIGHT •
Take the minimum amount weights that you require to help you descend.

STEP OUT •
Take a deep breath, and a big step out away from the side and enter the water vertically, feet first.

—————— Step 1 ——————

JUMP ENTRY

This method of entry can be done from the side of a pool, a jetty, or a large boat – anywhere where you will be steady and well supported before jumping. It must be carried out in water that is at least 2m (6½ft) deep. Take one breath through your snorkel, and then take the plunge. Remember you must come back to the surface before you attempt a surface dive.

Flat feet for a shallow drop

Pointed toes for a high drop

BUOYANCY •
The air in your lungs and the **buoyancy** of your wetsuit should ensure that you manage to surface again providing you do not have too many weights on your belt. Come up holding your breath and clear your snorkel back at the surface.

LEGS AND FINS •
After you have jumped, try to keep your legs straight and fairly close together. As you start to rise, slowly beat your fins to help you move back up to the surface of the pool.

Step 2
SURFACE DIVES

Once you are back on the surface, get used to swimming along face down using your basic equipment. Then, attempt a surface dive, or "breath-hold" dive. To begin the dive lie flat over water about 3m (10ft) deep.

LEGS
Put your legs above you in the air, and their weight will help you down. If necessary, you can pull with your arms to help you under. Start to fin once your fins have gone below the surface.

BEND •
Take a deep breath, and bend forward from your waist.

• FLIP UP
Flip your legs straight up and out of the water, using your arms to help pull you underwater.

• TURN
Turn upward to ascend, extending your arms and arching your back. As you come around, raise your face towards the surface.

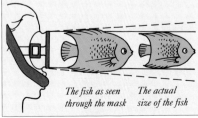

UNDERWATER SIGHT

A mask is a necessity to help your vision, which would otherwise be distorted underwater. The faceplate amends this distortion, allowing you to see distinctly. However, wearing the mask causes light rays to refract as they pass from water to air so that underwater objects look larger and closer than they actually are. You will soon adjust to this.

The fish as seen through the mask   *The actual size of the fish*

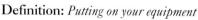

2 SUITING UP

Definition: *Putting on your equipment*

DAY 1

NOW THE BIG MOMENT has arrived, it is time to put on your **scuba** ready to take the plunge. All your diving equipment is safe, secure, and foolproof, and before you reach this stage, you must have a sound knowledge of how it all functions, and what each part of it is called. To suit up, you need to be wearing your wetsuit, and have with you a full tank, your **BC**, your **regulator**, weight belt and weights, and, of course, your mask and fins. You will appreciate the help of a co-diver, with whom you will execute a **pre-dive check**.

OBJECTIVE: To be fully prepared to dive safely. *Rating* •••

Step 1

ATTACHING AIR

Attach your **BC** to your tank on the side that the air exits. Put the **first-stage** on your tank, and clear the air valve. Take care that the exhaust ports are below your mouthpiece when you put the **second-stage** on. If not, move the first-stage until correctly placed, or your mouthpiece will be upside down. Push the filter guard into the **O-ring** groove and tighten the screw.

*O-ring:
check for
damage*

CLEAR AIR VALVE
Turn your tank quickly on and off, letting a puff of **compressed air** clear away any water or dirt from the valve.

AIR SUPPLY •
Breathe into your mouthpiece checking that the needle on the gauge is steady.

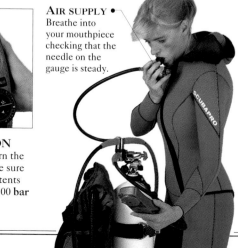

FIRST-STAGE
To fit the **first-stage**, place the **regulator A-clamp** over the **pillar valve**, with the filter over the **O-ring**.

SWITCH ON
When you turn the tank on, make sure that your contents gauge reads 200 **bar** (3000lb/in²).

Step 2
INTO GEAR

Ensure that your **BC** is connected properly. Pull the collar back on the **direct feed** tube and push it into its fixing, snapping the collar home. Now, press the inlet button to make certain that you can inflate the jacket with **compressed air** from your tank. Next, put on the jacket along with the tank and stand up. Make sure that all of your straps are fastened securely, and you know where all quick-releases are to be found. Place your weight belt so that it will fall free easily if you release it. Put on your fins and have your mask ready. Conduct a thorough **pre-dive check** with your co-diver.

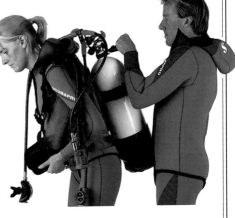

PUT ON THE TANK
If you have no support, your co-diver can help by lifting the tank so that you can simply slip your arms through your **BC**.

STAND UP •
Lean your head back to check that your tank is not sitting too high up on your back.

PRE-DIVE CHECK
Once all of your equipment has been fitted, you must get your co-diver to double check. Make sure that you are switched on and all your quick-releases and straps are secure, visible, and easy to reach. Now, make a final check of both your contents gauges, ensuring that they are full. Put your mask and fins on.

YOUR CO-DIVER
In open water and in the pool you will have a co-diver, with whom you must maintain contact until you are back on dry land.

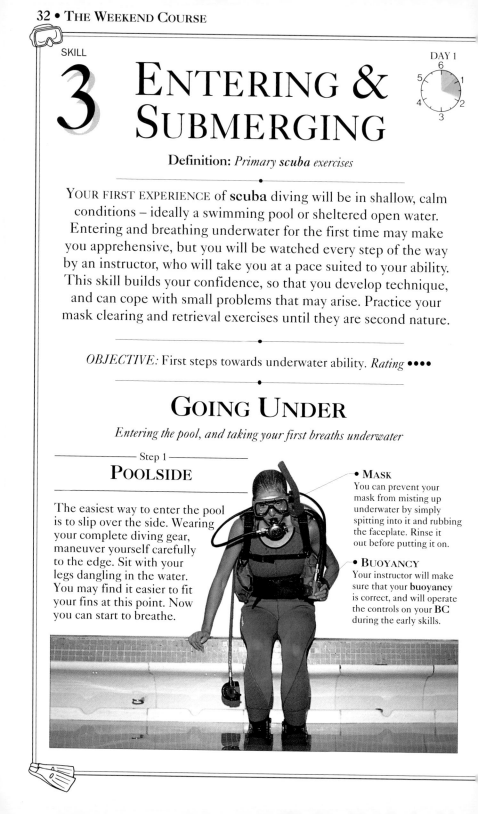

3 ENTERING & SUBMERGING

Definition: *Primary scuba exercises*

YOUR FIRST EXPERIENCE of **scuba** diving will be in shallow, calm conditions – ideally a swimming pool or sheltered open water. Entering and breathing underwater for the first time may make you apprehensive, but you will be watched every step of the way by an instructor, who will take you at a pace suited to your ability. This skill builds your confidence, so that you develop technique, and can cope with small problems that may arise. Practice your mask clearing and retrieval exercises until they are second nature.

OBJECTIVE: First steps towards underwater ability. *Rating* ••••

GOING UNDER

Entering the pool, and taking your first breaths underwater

Step 1
POOLSIDE

The easiest way to enter the pool is to slip over the side. Wearing your complete diving gear, maneuver yourself carefully to the edge. Sit with your legs dangling in the water. You may find it easier to fit your fins at this point. Now you can start to breathe.

• MASK
You can prevent your mask from misting up underwater by simply spitting into it and rubbing the faceplate. Rinse it out before putting it on.

• BUOYANCY
Your instructor will make sure that your **buoyancy** is correct, and will operate the controls on your **BC** during the early skills.

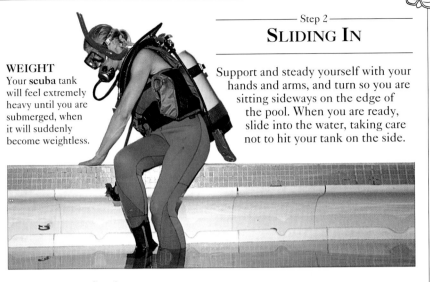

Step 2

SLIDING IN

WEIGHT
Your **scuba** tank will feel extremely heavy until you are submerged, when it will suddenly become weightless.

Support and steady yourself with your hands and arms, and turn so you are sitting sideways on the edge of the pool. When you are ready, slide into the water, taking care not to hit your tank on the side.

Step 3

HEAD UNDER

Starting in shallow water, lean forward bending at your knees and exhaling. Breathing out makes you less buoyant and if you have the correct weights on, you will find that you will sink effortlessly to your knees. Accustom yourself to the sensations of breathing underwater. Once you feel confident, you can start finning in the shallows.

SWAPPING SIGNALS
At the bottom of the pool, you must swap a firm OK signal with your co-diver and instructor. Form a circle with your thumb and forefinger, extending the rest behind.

EAR CLEARING

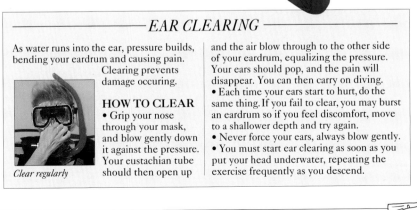

As water runs into the ear, pressure builds, bending your eardrum and causing pain. Clearing prevents damage occuring.

HOW TO CLEAR
• Grip your nose through your mask, and blow gently down it against the pressure. Your eustachian tube should then open up

Clear regularly

and the air blow through to the other side of your eardrum, equalizing the pressure. Your ears should pop, and the pain will disappear. You can then carry on diving.
• Each time your ears start to hurt, do the same thing. If you fail to clear, you may burst an eardrum so if you feel discomfort, move to a shallower depth and try again.
• Never force your ears, always blow gently.
• You must start ear clearing as soon as you put your head underwater, repeating the exercise frequently as you descend.

MASK CLEARING

Ensuring you can empty your mask of water

Step 1
FILL MASK

Kneel on the bottom of the pool
and concentrate on breathing through
your mouth. Gently pull the top rim
of your mask away from your head –
water will pour in – stop when the
mask is half-full. Continue to breathe
through your mouthpiece as normal.

Step 2
DRAIN MASK

Press your fingers against the top
of your faceplate, sealing it against
your forehead to prevent any air
from escaping. The next breath you
take blow out through your nose, and
into the mask. Air will fill your mask,
expelling the water out of the bottom
of it. Lean your head back slightly,
so that the water can drain out.

BLOW OUT
As you blow through
your nose, try to exhale
all the air in your lungs.
If you do not manage to
clear your mask the first
time you blow, take a
second breath and try
again. You may find this
exercise takes practice.

CONFIDENCE
Mask clearing is one
of the most important
skills that you have
to accomplish,
as it proves that you
will not panic if you trap
water in your mask. With
experience, this situation
will not present you with
any problem. You will
just lean your head back
as you swim, push in the
top rim, and blow out.

MOUTHPIECE REMOVAL

Removing and replacing the mouthpiece

Step 1
REMOVAL

Removing your air supply is a useful preliminary for the skill of sharing air (see pp.40-41). On the bottom, take a deep breath and hold it. Remove your mouthpiece. If it starts to bubble, turn it so that it is faces the bottom.

Step 2
REPLACEMENT

Replace your mouthpiece and breathe out. The action of exhaling when you replace your **regulator** clears any water that may have entered, so you should not get any stray drops of water in your mouth. Carry on breathing normally through your mouthpiece.

REGULATOR RETRIEVAL

If you ever run out of your own air supply, you will need to be able to remove your **regulator** to take somebody else's. Repeat the action of removal and replacement several times; when you feel confident, the next step is to release your air supply altogether. Locate, retrieve, and replace it, to carry on with normal breathing.

LETTING GO
Release and drop your mouthpiece so that it hangs down on the right-hand side of your body.

FINDING
When you want to continue breathing, hook your right arm backward so that you snag the breathing tube.

REPLACING
Take hold of your **regulator** mouthpiece, and put it back. Exhale, and then continue to breathe as before.

SKILL

4

ABILITY & MOBILITY

DAY 1

Definition: *Exercises to build proficiency with your scuba*

Move into water that is not shallower than 2m (6½ft), preferably 3m (10ft), deep. Going down and coming up are the most critical parts of a dive, and it is important that you have your movements and speed under control. Operation of your BC will help you but initially, practice exercises without using it. Try to start your descent without unduly disturbing the surface – in open water fish may be frightened by splashing. You can go down either head or feet first; ensure you have just enough weights on to enable you to sink.

OBJECTIVE: To gain confidence and skill in deeper water. *Rating* •••

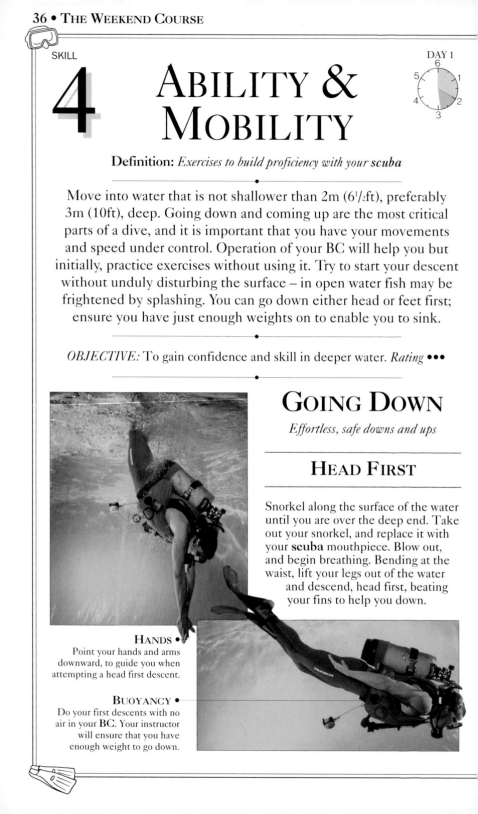

GOING DOWN

Effortless, safe downs and ups

HEAD FIRST

Snorkel along the surface of the water until you are over the deep end. Take out your snorkel, and replace it with your **scuba** mouthpiece. Blow out, and begin breathing. Bending at the waist, lift your legs out of the water and descend, head first, beating your fins to help you down.

HANDS •
Point your hands and arms downward, to guide you when attempting a head first descent.

BUOYANCY •
Do your first descents with no air in your **BC**. Your instructor will ensure that you have enough weight to go down.

FEET FIRST

In low visibility it may be safer for you to approach the bottom using a feet first method, so you must know how to go down in this way. Adopt a vertical position at the surface, with your mouthpiece in. Using your fins and arms to help, lift yourself up and out of the water as far as you can, with your fins pointing down. Breathe out, and sink. Once you are below the surface, you can then turn over into a head first position, and begin to fin.

POSITION •
Fin in a vertical position with your head above the surface.

• BODY AND LEGS
When you lift yourself, try to keep your body in a straight line with your legs as close together as possible. You can use your fins and arms to propel you up through the surface, and back under, before turning to make your descent.

• BEND AND TURN
When you are comfortably submerged, bend at your knees and then turn so that you are in a head first position. Facing towards the bottom, descend in a straight line.

COMING UP

When you come back up to the surface after diving, your ascent must always be performed carefully, and under control. Once the decision has been made, you must exchange the "let's go up" signal with your partner. Swim up facing each other, glancing at the surface, and also all around you to check for any hazards. As you break through the surface, do a quick 360° turn to check once more for obstacles. In the open water you may retain the mouthpiece, but practice changing back to your snorkel so you are able to do so if necessary (see p.45).

EAR CLEARING •
Clearing your ears is essential with every method of descent. Descend feet first all the way to the bottom if you have trouble with this.

SKILL 4 ROLLING

Rolls to improve your mobility and confidence in your scuba

FORWARD ROLL

Start by swimming fairly close to the surface. Bend at the waist and pull the water towards you with both hands. Without using your fins and trying not to twist your body, turn yourself over in the water until you have returned to your starting position. Progress to backward rolls when you are able to perform forward rolls confidently.

• **WAIST BEND**
To begin your roll, bend at the waist, as you would if you were performing a surface dive.

—PRESSURE EFFECTS—

Pressure affects masks

SQUEEZE
If you breathe in momentarily through your nose, pressure in your mask may fall causing it to suck against your face. Blow out gently through your nose if this happens.

PREVENTING LUNG DAMAGE
Your **regulator** feeds air to you at the same pressure as the water in which you are diving. This makes it easy for you to breathe naturally underwater. However, if you take a deep breath at the bottom and come up, holding your breath, this air in your lungs will remain at the same pressure. Due to the laws of physics, (pp.16-17), the air would expand as you ascended, and could result in a serious condition called **burst lung**. To prevent damage, breathe normally all the way to the surface.

• **STRAIGHT LEGS**
Keep your legs straight and static throughout the roll. Try to hold them as close together as possible and you will find that this exercise is much easier to complete.

CHANGING POSITION
Practicing these rolls will instill in you the confidence that your breathing apparatus has the ability to function in every position – even when you are upside down! Initially, practice the rolls close to the surface, and move to a midwater position when you feel more sure of your maneuverability.

MOVING AROUND
Attempt to use your arms, rather than your fins to propel you forward and round. Ideally you will return to your original position, so keep the rest of your body rigid, and try not to twist it as you move or you will find that you do not complete the roll correctly.

BACKWARD ROLL

Swim up towards the surface with your head back and your hands held in front of you. Place your palms forward and fingers upward. With enough depth beneath you, lean your head back. Use your palms to push up against the water.

- **LEG POSITION**
Attempt to keep your knees bent and your legs tucked up behind you during the course of your backward roll.

MOVEMENT
Develop your arm motions so that you are arching back in a circular movement. Keep your fingers together to help push you through the water.

- **BODY**
As with the forward roll do not twist your body as you move.

PUSH UP •
Force against the water to push up – you don't want to hit the bottom.

BARREL ROLL

As you move along in midwater, throw yourself into a corkscrew turn so that you swing through 360°. You can use your hands to help with the roll if necessary, as this maneuver may require some practice.

SURFACE CHECK
Practice the barrel roll until you can do it smoothly and effortlessly. It is a useful skill, as it enables you to check the surface above you without stopping, which is something you must do as you prepare to ascend.

LINE •
Try to maintain a horizontal line throughout this roll, so that you can continue to fin along as soon as you come out of the maneuver. If you keep your legs straight and together, you will find that this roll is much more easy to achieve.

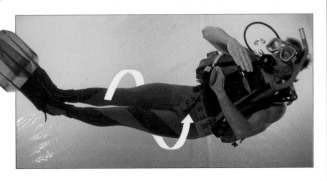

SKILL

4

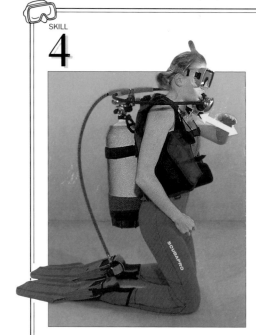

SHARING AIR

Methods of sharing mouthpieces

— Step 1 —

SIGNAL & APPROACH

To prepare for the unlikely situation in which your co-diver does not have an **octopus rig**, you must practice air sharing with one mouthpiece. Kneel on the bottom of the pool and make the "I have no air" signal – a chopping motion against the neck. As quickly as possible, your companion must come over to you, and stop at a right-angle close to your right-hand side.

• RIGHT SIDE
Your **second-stage** normally comes over your right shoulder, so your companion needs to be on this side.

— Steps 2 & 3 —

ONE MOUTHPIECE

Your co-diver takes a breath in, holds it, then they hand their mouthpiece to you. Breathe in once from your own set, remove it, and take the other mouthpiece. Breathe out into it, then take one breath in. Exhale, then take a second breath in and hold it. Now return the mouthpiece to your donor.

BREATHING RHYTHM
Remember to take two breaths each, always breathing in before handing over the **second-stage**. Exchange until you are satisfied that you can share air without difficulty. You must alternate in the role of the "distressed diver".

A FIRM GRIP
Always keep hold of your mouthpiece while another diver is breathing from it so you can take it back from them if you need to. If you don't do this you could end up without an air supply.

Step 4
USING AN OCTOPUS

Now try another method of sharing air using an **octopus rig**. Signal that you are out of air. Your co-diver locates his octopus and swims over, holding it in position. Remove your mouthpiece, replacing it with the octopus. Breathe out into it and continue to breathe. After taking ten breaths, relocate your mouthpiece, and breathe normally.

• PURGE VALVE
As your co-diver swims towards you they will keep their **purge valve** depressed to provide positive air pressure.

Steps 5 & 6
ON THE MOVE

Once you feel confident about all the methods of sharing air while in a static position, start using the **octopus rig** as you are moving. Then try sharing the same air supply while you are ascending – a vital safety procedure.

BUOYANCY CONTROL
Sharing air while you are on the move takes practice, especially as you may have to adjust your **buoyancy** to match that of your co-diver. If this differs drastically, you may not be able to maintain contact with ease. With more knowledge of your **BC**, a perfect level of buoyancy will be easier to achieve.

ASCENDING
If you are rising when waiting for the **octopus rig** to be passed to you, breathe out a little air to prevent any damage to your lungs. Beat your fins slowly to make your ascent.

SKILL

5 BUOYANCY CONTROL

DAY 1
6
5 1
4 2
3

Definition: *Using a BC to maintain **buoyancy** and control ascents*

ADJUSTING YOUR **BUOYANCY** at the touch of a button is one of the pleasures of diving, and is also vital when you are swimming over fragile coral reefs that could be damaged by your fins or knees. With correct buoyancy, there is also less chance of you colliding with the bottom and injuring yourself. You can already alter your buoyancy by breathing, and your instructor will have adjusted your weights to as near the ideal as possible. Now, you can practice using your **BC**.

OBJECTIVE: Controlling **buoyancy** and ascents safely. *Rating* ••••

MAINTAINING BUOYANCY

*Using **neutral buoyancy** to help you swim and hover underwater*

———— Step 1 ————
BOTTOM BALANCE

Practice this exercise until you are able to gauge just how much air you need to let in to adjust your upward motion without becoming vertical in the water. Swim to the bottom of the pool, and lay in a face down position.

FINS •
The aim of this **buoyancy** exercise is to control your upward progress so that your fins do not leave the bottom of the pool.

LEGS •
Once you are at the bottom of the pool you will need to place your legs and fins slightly apart, so that you can use them to support and balance you.

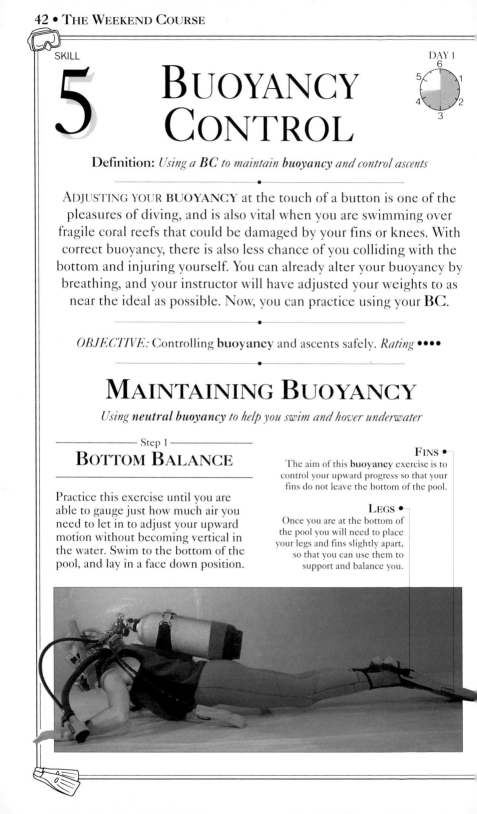

• Air In
Let in puffs of air, removing your
finger from the button each time.

Steps 2 & 3
Up and Down

Press on the inflation button once or
twice to let puffs of **compressed air**
into your jacket. After a few puffs, you
will begin to rise, try to keep your toes
on the bottom. When you start to rise,
hold the corrugated tube above you,
pressing the exhaust button. Air will
bubble out, and you will sink back
onto your front on the bottom.

Hose •
As you let air out of your **BC**
and sink towards the bottom,
hold the corrugated hose above
you so that it is situated in an
area that is of a lesser pressure.

Step 4
Midwater

With your left hand and fingers ready
to operate your **BC**, begin to move
along in midwater. As you advance,
let in air to make you lighter, and out
to make you heavier. Try not to make
any changes so severe that you arrive
at the surface or on the bottom.

CONTROLS

The buttons at the end of your **BC**
hose inflate or deflate your jacket
and make you appear more or less
buoyant. You use your fingers to
operate them and you should only
need to use one hand – usually
your left hand – to work these
buttons. Get used to "playing"
the BC controls like you would
a musical instrument.

Inflation control •
Exhaust control •

SKILL 5

SURFACING TECHNIQUES

Ascending safely, using your BC, and surface procedures

EXHAUST & INFLATE

You must let the air out of your **BC** as you ascend. If you fail to do this, the **compressed air** inside could expand and you would balloon up, returning to the surface out of control. The sort of ascent shown, allows you to come up safely. Start in a face down position on the bottom of the pool, and let small puffs of air into your BC so that you begin to rise. As your fins leave the bottom, bend and cross your legs. Use your exhaust and inflate buttons to regulate your ascent so that you rise gradually back to the surface.

• EXPANDING AIR
The most difficult part of this type of ascent is as you approach the surface, when expanding air in your **BC** tends to speed you up. Repeat the ascent several times, until you are able complete the last stage as slowly as possible.

• CROSS YOUR ANKLES
When attempting this controlled buoyant ascent, cross your ankles as you rise to deter you from using your fins. Learning to come up in this manner is useful, as it provides you with the confidence that you would be able to return to the surface without using your legs or fins, if you were suffering from a problem like cramp.

NATURAL BUOYANCY

You have a level of natural **buoyancy** that affects the weights you need to wear when you dive. If you tend to sink, you are "negatively buoyant", if you float upward you are "positively buoyant" and if you remain static, "**neutrally buoyant**".

CHANGES TO BUOYANCY
Certain factors affect your **buoyancy**:
• Your wetsuit – the thicker it is, the more buoyant you are, and the deeper you are the less buoyant it is.
• The volume of air in your tank.
• The number of weights you wear.

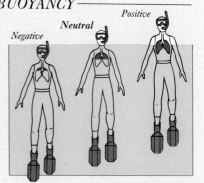

Negative *Neutral* *Positive*

DUMP & RISE

Practice another method of controlled ascent by using the **dump valve** on your **BC**. Place yourself in the start position on your front, on the bottom of the pool. Position your hands so that your left operates the inflation button. Your right hand operates the dump valve, a toggle that is found on the right-hand side of the jacket. Let air in using the inflation button, and control your rise by pulling the dump valve as necessary. You should aim to rise slowly, and under control.

• TRAPPED AIR
Air may get trapped in the right shoulder of your BC. If so, move so that the shoulder points down and the air will escape through the hose.

• FINS
Remember not to use your fins to help you ascend. The idea is to make the air in your BC work for you, giving you effortless support.

DUMP VALVE
Usually the **dump valve** is found just underneath the right shoulder of your **BC**. It is designed to allow you to halt any uncontrolled ascents by suddenly releasing a lot of air from the jacket.

CHANGE & SUPPORT

At the surface, you must learn how to change to breathing through your snorkel, and also how to inflate your **BC** for support. Hold your snorkel with your left hand, removing your **regulator** with your right. Put your snorkel into your mouth, blow out and start to breathe. To inflate your BC, follow the same sequence with your BC mouthpiece. Then, depress the exhaust button as you blow into your BC, releasing it after each puff.

INFLATING •
After 6 or 7 breaths your **BC** will be fully inflated.

SNORKEL •
Remember to take one last breath in from your **regulator** before you change to your snorkel.

6

DITCH & RETRIEVE

Definition: *Removing and replacing equipment underwater*

IT IS UNLIKELY that you will ever have to take off your **scuba** gear underwater. However, there is a remote chance that you might have to remove it in an emergency or if you became entangled in some way. "Ditch and Retrieve" raises your confidence, allowing you to become familiar with fastenings that you may have to adjust underwater. It is also useful practice for the times when you will have to take off and pass equipment up to a boat (see p.68). You should attempt this exercise in 2-3m (6½-10ft) of water.

OBJECTIVE: To remove retrieve, and refit the **scuba**. *Rating* •••••

─── Step 1 ───
LOOSEN & UNDO

By this stage you have gained a sound knowledge of, and confidence in your **scuba**. To start this sequence, swim down and kneel on the bottom of the pool. Unbuckle the waist and chest straps on your **BC**. However, do not remove your weight belt, as this will help you later in the skill, when you will have to perform a surface dive down to retrieve your equipment.

BUOYANCY COMPENSATOR •
Let enough **compressed air** out of your **BC** so that you are able to kneel comfortably on the bottom of the pool and not drift upward.

QUICK-RELEASES
The maneuvers shown here are made simpler by the quick-releases that are found on your **BC**. In an emergency, you would be able to remove your gear with speed and efficiency.

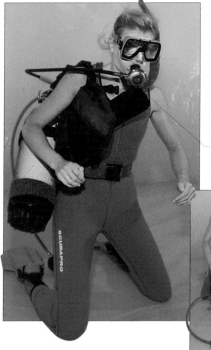

TAKE OFF

Next, take off your **BC** and **scuba**. Push your left hand through the left shoulder strap from behind. Pass your scuba tank and BC gently around to your right-hand side, remove them, and position them in front of you.

• **BREATHING**
Continue breathing steadily through your mouthpiece, all the time.

POSITION
With your mouthpiece still firmly in place, position your **BC** and **scuba** on the bottom of the pool, with the tank underneath. Keep close to your gear, as it will probably start to drift away from you. Be certain that there is hardly any air left in your BC, as this would cause your equipment to float, and it must remain static until retrieval.

AIR OUT

Remove your fins, then your mask, placing them near your tank. Take your mouthpiece out, stretching it away from the rest of your gear. As the first thing you will pick up when you come back, it must be distinct.

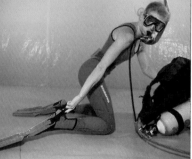

• **FINS**
Your fins may float when you remove them so while you are removing the rest of your gear it is a good idea to secure them, or signal to your co-diver to hold them until they need to be replaced.

• **MASK**
Take your mask off last, just before you remove your air supply. It will make the exercise much simpler for you if you are able to see exactly what you are attempting during the preceding stages.

SKILL

6

BREATHE OUT •
Breathe out as you rise
to prevent **burst lung**.

RISE UP

Once you have taken off the last item
of **scuba** equipment, slowly return to
the surface, remembering that you
must breathe out through pursed lips.
When you reach the surface, take
plenty of time to relax and catch your
breath. Identify your equipment on
the bottom of the pool in preparation
for going back down to retrieve it.

• A FREE ASCENT
This is the method that you would use to return
to the surface if you had no air left in your tank
and no companion nearby to come to your aid.

REST
With weights on, you will feel heavy treading
water, so before you dive back down, have a
rest and catch your breath at the poolside.

DIVE
After taking a
deep breath, dive
down to retrieve
your equipment.

Step 5

RETRIEVE & BREATHE

The first item you must recover when
you return to the bottom of the pool is
your air supply. You will be able to see
the shape of your mouthpiece and the
attached air hose stretching away from
your tank. With one hand, pick up your
mouthpiece, replace it, and start to
breathe, supporting the rest of your
gear with the other hand. If you have
a problem relocating your mouthpiece,
then make a **free ascent** and try again.

MOUTHPIECE
Check your **second-stage** is the correct
way up when you put it back in your
mouth, with the exhaust ports below
the rubber mouth grip.
Remember that you must
always exhale first when you
replace your mouthpiece.

• POSITION
Try to keep your
equipment upright.

MASK & FINS

Establish a normal breathing pattern
through your **regulator**. Now you can
begin to put on the rest of your gear.
Using your teeth, grip firmly onto your
mouthpiece. Keep your **scuba** steady
with one hand, and locate your mask.
Replace and clear it. As you are able to
breathe and see again, it will be easier
for you to replace your remaining gear.

• CLEAR MASK
After you have replaced
your mask you must clear it
immediately. With your head
tilted up and back, press in
the top rim, and then blow
out through your nose
pushing the water out.

REFIT

Finally, replace your jacket, putting
your right arm through the armhole.
Steady your tank with your right hand
as you put the left one through and
move it carefully across your back.

FASTENINGS
When you put your **scuba**
back on, you must make
sure that all of the straps
on your **BC** are straight
and have not become
twisted. Your air supply
tube must fall over the
correct shoulder. This
is usually your right side.

STAGE-BY-STAGE

• The "Ditch and Retrieve" exercise may
seem complicated, so it is a good idea if
you attempt it a stage at a time. Your
instructor will coach you through the skill,
suggesting ways for you to make it easier.
• To begin, ensure that you are happy
operating underwater without your mask.
Take it off at the surface and drop it.
When it has settled at the bottom of the

pool, swim down, refit, and clear it.
• Practice a **free ascent**, wearing your
mask and fins as aids, before attempting
the procedure without them.
• Next practice taking off your tank and
refitting it on the bottom of the pool.
• As your ability increases, add to the
amount of stages you do, until you can
complete the whole sequence smoothly.

SKILL

7 RECOVERY

DAY 1

Definition: *Recovering a distressed diver from underwater*

DIVING IS A SAFE SPORT, but there is always the possibility that something will go wrong. This will not usually be due to deficient equipment, but rather because human error or physical failure has occurred. It is vital that you can cope with such emergencies. If your co-diver has lost consciousness, they may eventually lose their mouthpiece, and in such a situation it is essential that you are able to act instantly and can return to the surface safely to recover. These resuscitation exercises must be learned properly by novice divers in the pool in preparation for possible open water emergencies.

OBJECTIVE: Recovery and resuscitation of a victim. *Rating* ••••

─── Step 1 ───
BUOYANT LIFT

Approach the victim taking hold of the right-hand side of their **BC** with your left hand. Hold their hose with your right hand, and start to let air into their BC. Keep the hose upright, so that you are able to operate the exhaust button if you rise too quickly. Ascend, under control, to the surface.

OPPOSITE •
Rise face-to-face, so you can watch the victim, and can replace their mouthpiece if necessary.

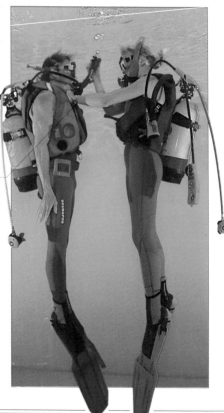

── *COMING UP FOR AIR* ──

Human error is the main factor in diving emergencies; they are usually caused by lack of air, because you have neglected to look at your contents gauge or have ignored the 50 **bar** (725lb/in^2) mark. If you are mobile and conscious, the best way to return to the surface is by sharing another diver's air. Ascend using the basic techniques shown on pp.40-41. Another method you can use is a **free ascent**, which is dealt with on p.55.

Step 2
ABOVE WATER

You should arrive back at the surface calm and ready to help your casualty. Let air into their **BC**, so that they are well supported, and inflate your own until you are buoyant and relaxed. Ideally, the victim should be positioned on their back, with their head clear of the water. If the casualty's breathing has stopped, you must immediately start to perform **expired air resuscitation** on the surface.

• BC
The **BC** should keep the casualty on their back with their head and mouth clear of the water. Remove their mouthpiece and mask.

• MOUTH
Fill the victim's lungs with air by blowing through their mouth.

Step 3
MOUTH-TO-MOUTH

For this resuscitation technique, seal the victim's nose, extending their neck and airway. Breathe in and place your mouth over the patient's. Inflate the lungs, 2 or 3 times, and then establish a rhythm of 10 puffs a minute.

SEAL •
Hold the casualty's chin, ensuring the airway is clear and extended.

HAND •
With this method you have to use one hand close the nose, but you may be able to get more air into the lungs.

MOUTH-TO-NOSE
In water the mouth-to-nose method may be easier to use as it allows you to keep one hand free so you can give the patient extra support. After each blow, release your hold and gently ease them to a floating position on their back.

— *SEEK ATTENTION* —

Obviously, in the swimming pool you will make your "We need help!" signal to an imaginary boat or shore party. If, however, you were in a real situation in open water you would continue to make the distress signal until it was responded to. In a situation such as this, it is probably best not to tow a casualty, unless there is no sign of help arriving, or you are close to the shoreline. You don't want to end up exhausted.

Stretch your arm straight up and wave it from side-to-side for help

SKILL

8 DECOMPRESSION

DAY 2

Definition: *Decompression sickness and the diver*

MOST OF THE AIR that you breathe consists of nitrogen. The deeper you travel underwater, the more nitrogen dissolves in your blood and fatty tissues. Consequently, if you remain underwater for too long and then return to the surface rapidly, your blood will be unable to contain the excess gas. The resulting bubbles that occur in your blood could block vital arteries, and cause varying degrees of damage. This condition is known as **decompression sickness (DCS)**, or "the bends". If you are aware of the symptoms and adhere to guidelines, the chances of getting it are minimal.

OBJECTIVE: To understand and know how to avoid **DCS**. *Rating* •••

SAFE PLANNING

Take care to plan every dive. Know the depth to which you will travel and the maximum time you can stay down. The longer and deeper your dive, the more you risk **DCS**. Your deepest dive should be your first of the day, and any successive dives shallower. Ascend slowly, 15m (50ft) per minute is recommended – the speed of your slowest exhaust bubbles.

—— SYMPTOMS ——

Most of the symptoms of **DCS** appear within an hour of you coming back to the surface. However, some may take up to 24 hours to appear. Symptoms are wide-ranging and variable. Those that you must be able to recognize include:
• Aches and pains in your joints, especially your shoulders and knees.
• Rashes or swellings.
• Nausea and vomiting.
• Numbness and tingling.
• Difficulty with breathing or standing.
• Confusion, convulsions, paralysis.
• Unconsciousness.

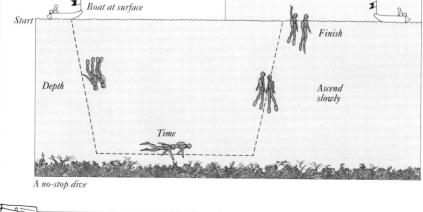

Start

Boat at surface

Finish

Depth

Ascend slowly

Time

A no-stop dive

KNOW YOUR LIMITS

All those responsible for divers must be acquainted with **decompression tables**. To plan dives safely and avoid **DCS**, tables or a dive computer (see p.78) must be used. These tell you how long you can safely stay under without doing **decompression stops**.

READING TABLES
Decompression tables for use by amateur divers have been developed by physiologists working for the world's navies. They are available from all major diving associations.

MAKING STOPS
A stop of at least 1 minute at 6m (20ft) on your ascent is recommended, to allow the elimination of nitrogen. Ideally, sport divers should not do dives that require longer stops.

CHAMBERS
Any diver who shows symptoms of **DCS** or **burst lung**, must be taken to a chamber. Transport chambers are now available so that divers may be taken, under pressure, to the larger chambers.

Compressed air and oxygen tank

TREATMENT

The only effective way to treat **DCS** is in a **recompression chamber**. The patient breathes oxygen using a mask, and is recompressed. They are then gradually decompressed back to normal **atmospheric pressure** so that the nitrogen bubbles do not reappear.

A folding portable chamber

SKILL

9 PREVENTION & CURE

DAY 2

Definition: *Emergencies and the problems of deeper diving*

YOU MAY FIND THAT you take naturally to the sensations of being underwater; but some feel anxiety, even in calm surroundings. Diving should be enjoyed – never dive if you feel unhappy about your circumstances, your equipment, or your physical condition. A number of small problems can quickly become a large one, leading to acute anxiety, stress, and panic. If you have awareness of what leads to these feelings, you will be a safer diver. You must also be acquainted with the specific problems that come with deeper diving, particularly the condition known as **nitrogen narcosis**.

OBJECTIVE: To know how to react in stressful situations. *Rating* •••

CAUSES FOR CONCERN

Recognizing warning signs and coping with a panicking diver

REASONS FOR PANIC

Cold, depth, low visibility, and strong currents, can all cause apprehension. This is exacerbated if you have little confidence in your dive leader; their concern should start before the dive – good planning, and an emphasis on relaxation and safety are paramount. With fear, behavior starts to become instinctive, and normal procedure is forgotten. If you notice irregularities in posture or breathing, suspect panic.

INDICATIONS OF FEAR
If a co-diver is surrounded by a mass of exhaust bubbles, their breathing may have become shallow and quick. If they also suddenly adopt a vertical position, using jerky strokes to move, suspect panic and prepare to take some emergency measures.

TAKING CONTROL

A panicking diver may try to head for the surface too rapidly, holding their breath. If you believe this is about to happen, move close to the person. Attempt to pacify them, before moving back up a shallower depth. Make an ascent as swiftly as you can, safely and under control.

KEEP IN CONTACT

Communication is essential when dealing with a panicking diver. Ascend so that you are facing each other and maintain eye contact, while reassuring them. Make firm and frequent OK signals, and ensure that they are always quickly reciprocated.

ON THE SURFACE •
Inflate your companion's
BC, and then your own.

EMERGING UNSCATHED

Always be a good companion. Ensure you have the ability to cope in emergencies:
• Learn all the necessary distress signals.
• Help a diver in difficulty, but try not to endanger or risk your own life.
• If your co-diver becomes unconscious, ascend letting air into their **BC**, or failing that, into your own (see pp.50-51).
• On land if there is no sign of breathing, start **artificial respiration** (see p.21).
• If symptoms start to appear that are not due to panic or shock, treat the victim with oxygen. Rapidly transport them to a **recompression chamber** (see p.53).
• Be sure that you are able to perform all the methods of air sharing (see pp.40-41).

A FREE ASCENT

If you you run out of air and are separated or too far away from other divers to share air, remember that you can return to the surface making a **free ascent**. Swim up steadily, blowing air out continuously from pursed lips, as when you practiced the "Ditch and Retrieve" exercise (see p.48).

DEEP DIVING

Nitrogen Narcosis and the perils of deeper diving

NARCOSIS

When you do a deep dive you increase the risks you take. One of the greatest problems caused by deep diving is a condition called **nitrogen narcosis** and you must be able to recognize and deal with any symptoms of this hazard. Induced by breathing nitrogen under pressure, the effects are quite similar to those of alcohol, causing confusion and slowing you down.

DOWN THE LINE
A **shot line** is anchored to the sea bed with a large buoy on the surface. You can dive down the line using it as a reference point.

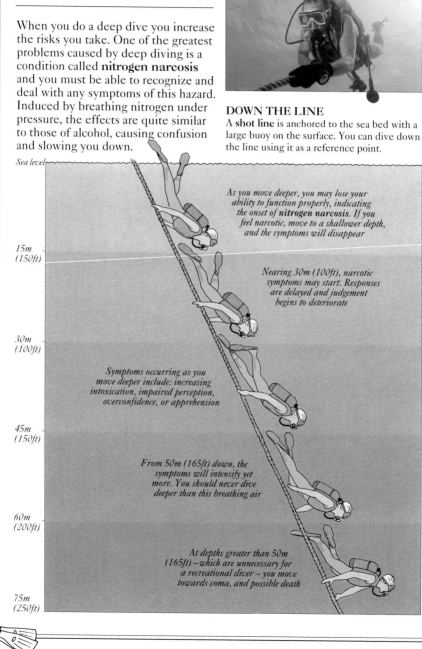

Sea level

As you move deeper, you may lose your ability to function properly, indicating the onset of **nitrogen narcosis.** *If you feel narcotic, move to a shallower depth, and the symptoms will disappear*

*15m
(150ft)*

Nearing 30m (100ft), narcotic symptoms may start. Responses are delayed and judgement begins to deteriorate

*30m
(100ft)*

Symptoms occurring as you move deeper include: increasing intoxication, impaired perception, overconfidence, or apprehension

*45m
(150ft)*

From 50m (165ft) down, the symptoms will intensify yet more. You should never dive deeper than this breathing air

*60m
(200ft)*

At depths greater than 50m (165ft) – which are unnecessary for a recreational diver – you move towards coma, and possible death

*75m
(250ft)*

GOING DEEPER

The time may come when you decide to broaden your experience to include a deeper dive. This must not be done casually. As the risks greatly increase, it is essential that careful plans are made, and that the details are clear to everybody involved. Build up to your target depth, making a series of dives, that increase your depth day-by-day.

PLAN YOUR DEPTH •
Never exceed your planned depth, as it could be extremely dangerous.

GAUGES •
Make sure your gauges are reliable, and accurate before you dive.

RECOGNIZING SYMPTOMS
It is important that you are able to recognize if a co-diver is suffering narcotic symptoms. Swap OK signals, ensuring they are clearly responded to. Close to a co-diver, you can also check their eyes, as the condition may produce a glazed look with dilated pupils.

EFFECTS OF THE DEEP

CURING NARCOSIS
Make sure you fully understand **nitrogen narcosis,** and that you know what to do if it should occur in yourself, or in a fellow diver. Never take any unnecessary risks.
• As with alcohol, narcosis affects younger people more acutely. Stay aware, as you have to be able to think when underwater, and keep your mouthpiece in place.
• If you feel the onset of symptoms, swim up to a shallower depth where they will disappear. There will not be after effects, but do not go deep on the same dive.
• As this condition is potentially fatal, you must never ignore any milder symptoms.

Night dives must be relatively shallow, as the risk of nitrogen narcosis increases in dark waters

OTHER EFFECTS OF DEPTH
Approach deep diving with care. Planning, preparation, and practice are all vital. In addition to narcosis, there are some other problems that may occur. Watch out for them in yourself, and those you dive with.
• The chance of **decompression sickness** (see pp.52-53), must be considered when making deep dives. Avoid dives that will involve **decompression stops**.
• Loss of light at depth, and the inability to see the sea bed or the surface, can lead to apprehension, fear and panic.
• Your suit is squeezed at depth, reducing its thickness and making you feel colder. This squeezing also results in a loss of **buoyancy,** overcome by using your **BC**.
• With the increasing depth you require more air with each breath, to match the pressure of the surrounding water. Although often you are not aware of this, at 30m (100ft) your breathing efficiency is reduced by 50%, so that any serious physical effort can result in breathlessness.

10 SHORELINE DIVING

Definition: *Entering open water from the shore*

WHEN YOU ARE PROFICIENT in all your pool exercises, and thoroughly comprehend the theory involved, you are ready for open water. Your first real dive in open water is likely to occur in an area of calm sea. This dive represents a leap forward in your experience and training and, of course, it is vital that you are with an experienced instructor, who will guide you through this new and different environment. As in the pool, you will have a co-diver with whom you stay from the suiting up stage, until you exit the water.

OBJECTIVE: To enter open water, acclimatize, and exit. *Rating* •••

Step 1

ON THE BEACH

Before you enter the water, make sure that you are properly suited up. Carry out a thorough **pre-dive check** with your co-diver, ensuring that you have all your necessary equipment and that all connections are in place.

CHECK GAUGES •
Look at your contents gauges to ensure that the air pressure of both your tank and that of your partner, reaches 200 **bar** (3000lb/in²).

STRAP ON
Attach your knife to your calf with straps. When open water diving, it is a good idea to fit your snorkel behind these, so that it does not interfere with your mask in any way.

Step 2
FITTING FINS

Approach the water's edge and step in. Put your fins on while you are still in the shallows. To do this efficiently you will need to find a stable prop – your co-diver is a good choice for this.

Steps 3 & 4
SHUFFLING IN

When you are completely equipped, start to breathe freely through your mouthpiece. Now you are ready, begin your shuffle backward into the sea. The advantage of moving in this position is that you are much less likely to stumble over your fins.

OVER THE SHOULDER
Glance over your shoulder as you shuffle in to check that there is nothing obstructing your path and there is no sudden surf surge.

Step 5
GOING UNDER

As the water rises up your body, the weight of your tank will disappear. After your **buoyancy** check, stand up again and then begin your dive.

BUOYANCY CHECK
When the water is up to your chest make a final **buoyancy** check. With no air in your **BC**, lean forward and breathe out; you should gently sink.

• SIGNAL
Both you and your partner must use a clear and positive OK signal, followed by "let's go down" – the thumb jerked downward – before you start your descent.

SKILL

10

—————Step 6—————
DESCENDING

Descend slowly with your co-diver following the natural slope of the sea bed. Remember to check your depth gauge frequently, so that you are aware of your position. It is very unlikely that you will be taken much further than 6m (20ft) deep on this initial dive.

EQUALIZE
Frequent **ear clearing** – equalizing – is an essential process during your descent. Simply hold onto your nose and blow gently and your ears should pop. If you find they will not clear straight away, come up to a shallower depth and repeat the procedure.

—————Step 7—————
MOVING ALONG

Swim along slowly and calmly, using only your fins. Relax and breathe steadily through your mouthpiece. Regularly adjust your **buoyancy**, avoiding any collisions with the sea bed. If you start to feel a little heavy, let a small puff of air into your **BC**. You must stay constantly aware of your environment, absorbing everything around you, as you move through it.

• SIGNALS
Remember that you must keep exchanging frequent OK signals as you progress on your dive. It is imperative that you maintain this form of contact with your instructor and partner from start to finish.

Steps 8 & 9
COMING UP

After a few minutes you will begin your ascent. The leader of your dive group makes the "let's go up" signal, and you and your co-diver do likewise. Swim slowly back up the slope of the shore, remembering to let air out of your **BC**.

Step 10
SHUFFLING OUT

When you reach shallow water, stand up and shuffle out, moving backwards until you are clear of the water. After your return from the dive, discuss it with your fellow divers, describing everything you saw, and any minor problems you may have encountered. All of this can be put in your **log book** (see p.74).

• EQUIPMENT
As you shuffle out, your equipment starts to feel heavy as it regains the weight it temporarily lost underwater. Don't worry as you will soon be able to remove it!

SKILL

11 BOAT DIVING

DAY 2

Definition: *Diving from large and small boats*

MANY OF THE BEST DIVES are to be found further from the shore, and can only be reached by boat. These boats may be quite large with lots of room on deck for changing into your gear, or small, in which case you may suit up before you depart from the shore.
Before you leave your boat you will have a thorough briefing, confirming necessary details such as the depth and time of the dive.
Each method of entry and exit, be it from a large or small boat, is shown, so that you can be prepared for the one that you need to use.

OBJECTIVE: To complete a dive from a boat. *Rating* •••

IN FROM ABOVE

Methods of entry from a big boat

A GIANT STEP

MASK •
Hold your mask, putting one hand across the faceplate.

To enter the sea from a large boat, a jump entry, as practiced in the pool, can be used. Check that there are no obstructions in the water. With your mouthpiece in, start breathing, steady yourself, and then take a giant stride.

IN THE AIR
You must keep yourself vertical while in the air. If your **BC** feels slightly loose, hold onto it with your free hand as you step off, to prevent it riding up your back on impact.

FEET •
Keep your feet parallel. Bring them back together after you have stepped out.

A FORWARD ROLL

Support yourself standing on a steady edge, at a height of not more than 1m (3ft) from the surface. Bend your knees slightly, in preparation to push off. Tuck your head into your chest, and look downward. When you are ready, spring off, and turn in the air so that your shoulders make contact with the water first. With both these methods of entry, relax after you have hit the water. The air in your **BC** will bring you back to the surface.

FACE •
Keep your mask secure against your face as you do a forward roll.

PUSH OFF •
Use the strength of your legs to help push you off the side and over.

EQUIPMENT •
You must be certain that all of your equipment is well secured before you make an entrance.

TUCK IN •
Keep your head tucked well in and do not look out towards the water as you leave the edge.

FLAT WATER
Until you are experienced you must always practice this method of entry in water that is flat and calm. Be certain that the other members of your dive group realize that you are going to perform a forward roll.

— PRE-DIVE CHECK —

As always, you must do a complete **pre-dive check** with your co-diver before you commence your dive:
• Be sure that you have all the gear you will need before you leave the shore.
• Remember to inflate your **BC** slightly before you make your entrance.
• Make sure your all quick-releases, are easily accessible and that all the valves and tubes are properly connected.

GOING IN BACKWARD

The standard roll entry performed from a small boat

SMALL BOATS

A typical route to open water diving is in a small boat. Low in the water, and easy to maneuver at close quarters, it serves as a ferry, taking you directly to your chosen dive site from a larger boat, or straight from the shoreline, from where they can easily be launched. They can also pick you up after your dive, from wherever you surface. You must take an anchor and paddles with you for use in case of engine failure, in addition to the standard safety equipment.

Dive organizer

INFLATABLE DINGHIES
Inflatables may look flimsy, but are efficient, strong, and fast sea boats.

CAPACITY
Small boats carry up to 8 fully suited divers. Sit opposite your co-diver, so that you can both leave at the same moment on the order of your dive organizer.

--- Step 1 ---

ON THE EDGE

SECURE MASK •
Hold your mask firmly against your head with one hand so that it does not fly off.

The most usual entrance method performed from a small boat or a dinghy, is a backward roll. After suiting up on the shore, enter your boat and sit, facing the middle, near to, or actually on, the side. Don't forget to run through a **pre-dive check** before rolling.

• CLEAR WAY
Check, or ask your co-diver to check, that the way is clear for you to roll backward without colliding with any other divers or obstructions.

Step 2
ROLLING OVER

Having finished all your checks, start to move yourself towards the edge of the boat. Inflate your **BC** slightly so that you float up easily. Bending your head forward, tuck it in to your chest. Relax, and when you are ready, on the signal from your dive organizer, roll gently backward into the water together.

• LIFT YOUR LEGS
To help elevate and propel your roll, lift your legs up so that they move out and well away from the boat.

AIR SUPPLY •
Keep your mouthpiece, as well as your mask secure throughout this maneuver.

Step 3
MAKING CONTACT

Try not to tense up when you make contact with the water. Keep your legs close together, and position the rest of your body so it is as compact and relaxed as possible. You will find that you do not sink far below the surface and, as you have already inflated your BC, you will rise immediately.

BREATHING
Remember not to hold your breath when you tumble backward and hit the water.

— SURFACE SIGNAL —

When you resurface after your roll, and before you start to dive, make the OK signal to your boat. The signal must be returned immediately.

• Hold up your arm so it is straight and clear of the water to signal OK

IN THE WATER
You will find that the water will feel pleasant and cool as you enter. When you surface after any type of entry, you must join up with your co-diver, make the required signals and then you can proceed with your descent and dive.

TROPICAL DIVE

Descending after your boat entry and diving through tropical water, ascending, and surfacing

—————— Steps 1 & 2 ——————
BELOW SURFACE

Let air out of your **BC** so that you can sink without effort. Descend at a shallow angle. Remember to clear your ears as you go down. Soon you will arrive at the sea bed, you will not be deeper than 10m (33ft). Try to maintain the correct level of **buoyancy**, and you will not need to use your fins to stay up or down.

• **WEIGHT**
To achieve **neutral buoyancy** in the sea, you need to wear more weights than you wore in the pool, as you are more buoyant in salt water than in you are in fresh water.

• **TWO-BY-TWO**
Stay with your co-diver, moving along the reef edge. The most interesting and colorful marine life is to be found here and it also provides a visual guide for the dive.

Step 3
FINISHING

Stay observant throughout your dive, noting any interesting features for your **log book**. Check your air supply frequently. When the contents needle reaches 50 **bar** (725lb/in^2), you must make the "short of air" signal to your fellow divers. This is followed with the signal for "let's go up".

STUDYING DIALS
You must remember to refer to your gauges during the course of your dive. Never exceed your planned depth, and always begin your ascent when the contents gauge of one of your group reaches the 50 **bar** (725lb/in^2) mark.

SHORT OF AIR
The signal that informs others you are short of air is made by forming an upright, clenched fist, facing forward.

Steps 4 & 5
SURFACING

Remember to come up slowly and carefully. Move no faster than your smallest air bubbles to avoid **DCS**. Travel up opposite your co-diver, and keep glancing above, to make sure there are no boats or any other obstructions at the surface. When you break the surface, inflate your **BC** to give you extra support.

• **FACE-TO-FACE**
Be certain that you maintain regular contact with your co-diver all the way to the surface not forgetting to use the recognized signals.

• **AT THE SURFACE**
The first thing to do when you arrive at the surface is signal to your boat party.

UP & OVER

Removing gear and getting back on to a small boat

Step 1
TAKING OFF

Prepare to pass your gear up to your boat. Take off your weight belt first, followed by your **BC**. Undo the waist and chest straps, and then maneuver yourself out of the armholes. Now, someone will lean over the side of the boat and lift your set away from you.

LOSING WEIGHT

First give your weight belt to a member of your boat party, as it will feel heavy back at the surface. Pass it up, making sure you hold it by the end without the catch. If you hold at the other end, the weights may slide off and end up sinking to the bottom of the sea.

BC •
Inflate your **BC** at the surface to provide you with some extra support.

• MOUTHPIECE
Before you pass up your **scuba** gear to the boat, remember that you must remove your mouthpiece.

FIN POWER •
Beating your fins up and down helps you gain the momentum to lift yourself.

Step 2
BOUNCING UP

Once all of the equipment has been taken up and stored in the bottom of the boat, you can get back on board. Holding firmly on to the edge of the boat, bounce up and down in the water until you can push yourself far enough up, so that you lurch over the side. Finally, remove your fins.

TURN
With a final push, heave yourself up and turn so that you sit on the edge of the boat facing outward, then swing your legs on board.

UP THE LADDER

Getting back on to a big boat still wearing your gear

—————— Steps 1 & 2 ——————

CLIMBING UP

Once the boat ladder is clear of other divers, someone will signal for you to go up. Swim to the ladder, and grab hold of it. It is set well away from the side of the boat, so that you do not have to take off your fins to climb it. You may feel unstable once you are back on deck, and so will probably need someone to assist you, as you remove all your equipment.

HELP AT HAND •
Someone on board will help you as you come up the rungs.

GRIP
Hold on firmly to the ladder, as you will find that it will take a fair amount of strength to pull yourself back up to the deck of the boat.

TANK •
Breaking through the surface you will feel the weight of your tank.

—————— *BACK ON BOARD* ——————

Once your dive is completed you will find that the first thing you will want to do is talk about it. However, there are certain things that you must always do first:
• If possible, you should rinse out all of your diving equipment in fresh water.
• Store all equipment so that it is safe and secure, is not obstructing anyone's path, or being a potential cause of accidents.
• Pack delicate items like your mask and instruments away in your dive bag, where they will not get trodden on and damaged.

YOUR LOG
Details of your dive can now be entered in a **log book** (see p.74). The dive can then go forward as a record of your experience and a step towards qualifying as a diver.

After the dive your dive leader or instructor will verify your dive for your **log book** *with their signature and the dive center's stamp*

SKILL

DAY 2

12 USING A MARKER BUOY

Definition: *Diving with a surface marker buoy (SMB)*

FOR ALL DIVES in currents or tides, and whenever there is even a faint chance of divers losing their way, it is essential that a member of your dive group uses a **surface marker buoy (SMB)**. This piece of equipment allows your cover boat to follow you during the dive, and be close by whenever you surface. This lesson teaches you to how to use a buoy correctly. You will make your descent with the buoy in shallow water of about 6m (20ft) deep, down to the sea bed, and then surface back to your cover boat shortly afterwards.

OBJECTIVE: A descent, short swim, and ascent with a **SMB**. *Rating* •••

TAKING THE BUOY •
A member of your boat party will pass down the **surface marker buoy** to you once you are comfortable in the water. The reel on the buoy will still be fully wound at this point.

GOING DOWN •
When all the members of your group are comfortable in the water and fully prepared, make the recognized "let's go down" signal, by jerking your thumb firmly down. Once everyone has replied, you begin your dive.

———— Steps 1 & 2 ————
ON SURFACE

Take hold of the **surface marker buoy**. It is usually held by just one diver in a group, but it can also be passed between divers. Once you are certain that all divers are OK, and are breathing normally from their mouthpieces, make the "let's go down" signal. Prepare to make your descent feet first and, as you leave the surface, release the catch on the reel of your SMB, so that the line can unwind easily.

LINE •
The line should rise
steeply towards the
surface all the time.

Steps 3 to 5
DOWN THE LINE

Start to sink feet first, away from your
buoy, using your **BC**. The remaining
divers in the group then follow the
line, head first, taking care not to pull
on it. At the bottom, trigger the catch
to prevent your reel from unwinding
and wait for the other divers in the
group to arrive, then start to move off.

• **DESCEND**	• **COMING UP**
Descend feet first	After a short swim make
remembering to	the "let's go up" to your
clear your ears	companions on the sea
as you go down.	bed and start to ascend.

Steps 6 & 7
TO THE SURFACE

After signalling, start to ascend. Begin
to wind in your **buoy**, rising slowly up
the line. Reel in the line so that it is
always taut. The rest of the divers will
follow you. Back at the surface, make
certain that your fellow divers are OK.
Next, signal to your boat, and it will
collect you from your new position.

OK •
Make a firm OK
signal at the surface.

POSITION •
Your co-divers face
inward, as you rise.

AFTER THE WEEKEND

What you can aspire to in your future as a diver

NOW YOU HAVE DONE all the exercises and dives set out in this book, you are well on the way to being a qualified diver. Make sure that your training continues with an instructor who is properly qualified, to a nationally, or internationally, recognized standard.

Read diving manuals, books, and magazines to broaden your horizons and give you new ideas. Once you have qualified, there are so many new and exciting diving experiences for you to enjoy. You will begin to acquire your own equipment – look after it. Courses will teach you new techniques such as rescue, boat handling, and navigation or to give you a background in marine biology, fish identification, underwater archaeology, or photography. Why not try cave and night diving – it will be unforgettable, but make sure that you dive with experienced companions who have planned properly, and avoid "macho" or "cowboy" divers. You will find every dive is different: you can soar over and down vertical walls and float weightless to admire colorful animals or ancient wrecks. However, remember that you must conserve this "new world", and that you do have limitations, so don't take unnecessary risks. If you follow all the rules, the underwater world is your oyster.

SCUBA SENSE

Detailing and recording your dives, and rules to remember

AS SOON AS YOU START open water diving, you should begin keeping a **log book**. The organization that you learn with may well provide you with one to record your qualifications and details of your dives. The essential information that you have to document is the date, place, depth, and time of each dive; you can also note everything that you saw and experienced. An instructor should verify each entry, adding a stamp, showing their qualification details, and the name of the dive center. The more you put into your dives, the more you will get out of them. The "Golden Rules" given here are the essence of all you have learned. Read and absorb them, and take care that they are observed every time you dive.

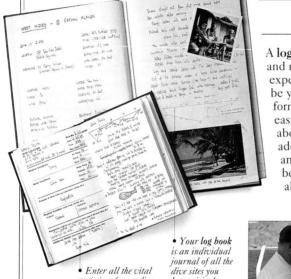

• *Enter all the vital statistics of your dive*

• *Your log book is an individual journal of all the dive sites you have visited*

LOGGING

A **log book** records all the essential and necessary proof of your diving experiences. However, it can also be your underwater diary. Larger formats, and blank page books are easily adapted so you can write about your dives at more length, add photographs, and draw maps and plans. Your log book then becomes a unique chronicle of all your sub-aqua experiences.

THE KEY TO DISCOVERY
Novice divers may not realize that what they have observed, particularly in an area that they have dived in regularly, could be of significant interest to a marine scientist or archaeologist. A small note or drawing in a **log book** may well lead you, or someone else, to an important underwater discovery.

"GOLDEN RULES"

The sea is not the natural environment of humans, and our time underwater is regulated. If you relax, keep energy in reserve for emergencies, and surface slowly, you will arrive in good shape. Always follow these "golden rules".

Don't forget to OK

BASIC RULES

• You must never dive alone. Ensure that you always have a qualified instructor with you, particularly for your first few dives.
• Never dive without a **BC**, or some other sort of **compressed air** life jacket.
• If you are going to be diving in a current, you, or another member of your group, must take an **SMB**.
• Avoid doing very deep dives, and any that involve **decompression stops**, unless they are carefully planned and you have plenty of diving experience.
• Remember that you must always plan your dive and follow that plan.

PRE-DIVE CHECK

• Do a proper **pre-dive check** with your companion before you enter the water.
• Make sure that all the quick-releases, air, and **BC** hoses are properly connected.
• Ensure that you and your co-divers have full tanks and are switched on.
• Check that your mask is comfortable and in place so that it will not leak.

• Confirm that you, and all those who dive with you, know and can respond to the group of recognized signals.
• Discuss your dive plan, confirm how you intend to enter and exit the water.

Contents gauge

DURING YOUR DIVE

• When you are wearing a new or different suit, check your weight in the shallows before you commence a dive. Never take any more weight than is necessary.
• Make sure that your **buoyancy** is properly adjusted.
• Practice your mask clearing in shallow water if you have not performed the exercise for some time.
• Start clearing your ears from the minute you leave the surface – *never* force them. If you start to feel any discomfort, come up slightly and try to clear again.
• Always keep close to your co-diver and dive group.
• Try to move with any currents, not against them.
• If your mask sucks onto your face, blow more air into it from your nose, to equalize the differing pressure.
• Do not try to lift heavy objects back to the surface.
• If you feel the onset of **nitrogen narcosis**, swim up to a shallower depth. Make certain your companion is responding to your signals quickly and efficiently.
• Be careful what you touch. You don't want to injure yourself or the natural inhabitants of the sea.
• Breathe freely as you ascend, *never* hold your breath. In an emergency carry out a **free ascent** (see p.55).

A free ascent

At ease on surface

AND FINALLY

Remember that the best diver is not the one who dives deepest, but the one who comes back most regularly. Don't take any unnecessary risks, and when you are back at the surface inflate your **BC** and simply relax. A good diver arrives alive!

EQUIPMENT & CARE

*Purchasing and maintaining **scuba** diving equipment*

DIVING SCHOOLS AND CLUBS usually provide you with the majority of equipment while you are learning to dive. As the equipment is expensive you will probably wish to acquire your own piece-by-piece, as you become more enthusiastic. Try to buy your underwater equipment from a recommended and reputable dive shop. Avoid buying from a general sports shop. Dive shops are usually run by enthusiastic divers or instructors who can give you advice. They will have gear in a variety of sizes. Don't buy equipment that is too large or too heavy for you – alternatives can be always be ordered if what you require is not in stock.

DETAILS

Every **scuba** tank should be regularly and stringently tested. Details that show manufacture, date, capacity, test and working pressure, weight and specifications are stamped onto every tank.

• *Pressure*

• *Hose*

• *Motor*

TESTING & FILLING

Tanks must be hydraulically tested every 4 years, visually tested every 2 and stamped to prove this. If you buy a second-hand tank, check that these conditions are imprinted. Tanks are filled from compressors. These are usually operated from dive centers or shops, although it is possible to obtain portable compressors.

• AIR
Air is taken from the atmosphere, compressed and then pumped into the tank by means of a flexible hose.

• MOTOR
Compressors are run on electricity or gas. If you use a gas motor, keep the air intake well away from the engine's exhaust. Ensure oil levels and filters are checked regularly.

MAINTENANCE

After getting your basic equipment such as mask, fins, and snorkel, you will probably find that the next item you want to purchase is a wetsuit. Unless money is no object, decide where you are going to do most of your diving, and choose a suit that is the appropriate thickness for the conditions there. Follow the care advice here and you will find your equipment will last you for years.

BC AND REGULATOR
Rinse out your **BC** after your dives. Inflate it by mouth after washing, and allow it to dry out away from the heat of the sun. You must also wash your **regulator,** but attempt to keep water out of the filter or it may be damaged.

WETSUITS
Equipment like wetsuits and masks is best rinsed in fresh water as soon as possible after use. Keep all rubber and **neoprene** items out of sunlight to prevent them from fading.

HANG IT UP
Always hang wetsuits up to dry so that fresh air can circulate around them. Do not pack them flat in a drawer or cupboard, as this will encourage them to rot. This advice is particularly important, if you are not going to be using your diving equipment for a while.

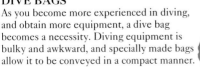

DIVE BAGS
As you become more experienced in diving, and obtain more equipment, a dive bag becomes a necessity. Diving equipment is bulky and awkward, and specially made bags allow it to be conveyed in a compact manner.

ADVANCING

More specialized diving equipment

BEFORE LONG YOU will want to understand and take responsibility for your dives, even if you are still accompanied by a dive guide or instructor. A safe and successful dive depends on careful planning and on reading and interpreting the instruments that inform you of your depth and time underwater. There is a variety of diving instruments you can choose from. Always take advice on what you need and make sure you choose wisely. Start with simple gauges, which you must use in tandem with a watch. Using these you have to rely on your memory, in order not to exceed a planned depth. Later, you can acquire more sophisticated digital depth gauges or computers, which will further aid your calculations.

INSTRUMENTS

All your instruments must be serviced regularly, as they will be frequently read during the course of your dives, and are vital to your safety. Initially, it best to acquire just a basic gauge with a needle, and a watch. Computers are considerably more expensive, but are able to perform the functions of both the gauge and the watch. Remember you will have to read a computer not only above water, but under it as well.

• **DIVING WATCHES**
As you leave the surface, move the zero mark, on the movable **bezel** on your watch, so that it is opposite the minute hand. This will enable you to read off the number of minutes you have been under quickly and easily, and know when it is time for you to begin your ascent.

DEPTH GAUGES •
Simple depth gauges work by water pressure pressing on the back of the case. This pushes the indicator needle over a graduated face, so that you can read off your depth. With these, you will have to remember your greatest depth.

CAREFUL PLANNING
With a digital depth gauge or computer, you should not have to do anything except read off figures, but it is still wise to plan your depth and time carefully before you leave.

• **COMPUTERS**
A diving computer allows you constant monitoring of dives. It can give you essential facts about the depth and time underwater and also details about safe rates of ascent or descent. If you want to dive again on the same day, a dive computer can calculate specific times so that, following its instructions, you know exactly *Time* • • *Depth* when to go back to the surface.

NAVIGATION

On your first dives, guides will follow the natural features of the sea bed to navigate and you will be amazed at their ability to bring you back to your starting point. Using a compass will give you a clearer idea of a position underwater, and the confidence that you can find your way back to base.

- *Direction slit*
- *Direction of travel arrow*
- *North seeking needle*
- *Calibration*
- *Bezel*

PLOTTING A COURSE
You will be taught navigation and compass skills thoroughly before you are given the actual responsibility of guiding dives.

THE DIVER'S COMPASS
Some compasses for divers are calibrated anti-clockwise – the opposite to a normal compass. They have a fixed direction of travel arrow that indicates the route you follow after you have fixed your bearing.

In front

On your wrist

USING BEARINGS
Move the **bezel** around until the direction slit matches your bearing. Rotate yourself until the needle is in the slit. Set off following the direction arrow.

NEEDLE AND ARROW
The needle of a compass will always point toward magnetic north. The direction of travel arrow is fixed and you follow it along your chosen course.

KEEP LEVEL
You can either take your compass off and hold it firmly in both hands flat in front of you, or keep it on your wrist, level and at right angles to your body. Your body should always align with the direction arrow.

—————— USING A COMPASS ——————

If you use a compass regularly, even to check its reading from time-to-time, you will have a much better idea of your position relative to a fixed starting point. There are various different situations in which a compass may be used.

- Taking a bearing on the surface on an object that you want to swim to.
- Following a particular bearing, for example 270°, towards a given location.
- Checking the compass and following a reciprocal bearing in order to return to your starting point.

WHAT NEXT?

Developing your experience and interests

ONCE YOU HAVE LEARNED the basics, you need to build up your experience and ability so that you can qualify to dive without an instructor and, perhaps even lead or teach diving yourself. You may want to specialize in a particular area of diving. Most organizations offer advanced courses in life saving, first aid, navigation and boat handling, as well as other subjects, such as marine archaeology or biology. Photography and video-making are two areas that enthuse and inspire many divers, and they provide personal and colorful records of what you have seen and experienced. It may be worth taking a course in either subject, so that you can improve your technical and creative abilities to increase your skill.

LEARN & EXPERIENCE

Diving is a sport that can take you all over the world. You may have begun your diving lessons in a tropical resort. If not, there are many dive centers in exotic places that you can visit to supplement pool training. Be certain that you choose to learn with a school or training center that is recognized, and you follow an approved course.

WHERE TO GO
Exotic locations like Eilat on the Red Sea provide ideal places for you to learn diving or increase your ability.

IN CLASS
Theory, as you will have realized, plays an essential part of your dive training. The time you spend in the classroom is as important as the time you spend underwater.

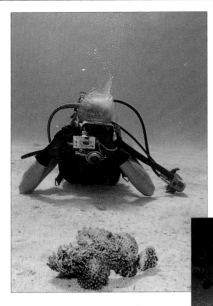

PHOTOGRAPHY

Photography allows you to bring back original images of your dives that will remind you of them for years to come. Taking good photographs underwater is not easy, although the equipment is becoming more simple to use. There are lightweight, amphibious cameras suitable for beginners now available. These range from cheap, disposable instant models, to the more advanced and expensive 35mm variety.

ADVICE

Take proper advice from an experienced photographer, and dive with them when you have rented or bought your own camera. You will find that photographers tend to move more slowly than the average diver, as they photograph the scenery.

IDENTIFICATION

Photography gives a reference point from which to identify undersea life.

MAKING MOVIES

For the more ambitious, video cameras for use underwater are now available. These allow you to take home films of each of your diving trips. Equipment of this type is not cheap but, fortunately, it is easily hired from good dive shops or centers.

STAYING DRY

Both still and video equipment can be housed in protective outer casings. These keep the cameras dry so that they can be used underwater. Most underwater cameras are **neutrally buoyant** in water.

—READ ALL ABOUT IT—

Most diving magazines include valuable information about clubs and contacts, as well as details about developments that occur in the world of diving.

Each of the world's major diving organizations produces its own relevant magazine. As well as giving you useful tips, they can inspire you to dive in different places

DIVERSE DIVES

Further underwater experiences: night and cave diving

ONCE YOU REALLY BEGIN to enjoy diving – the endless exploration and discovery, the feeling of weightlessness, and the satisfaction of using your hard-won pool techniques to build up your confidence – you will probably want to extend your diving experience into different areas. One of the first of these new adventures is likely to be a night dive. Nocturnal expeditions are frequently organized in tropical resort locations, where they can be more easily prepared as the conditions are ideally suited to this sort of dive. Diving in caves is another exciting option that you may want to investigate and is great fun. You will discover that both types of dive are inspirational but, as with every dive you make, they must always be done under the proper conditions and with the correct guidance.

CAVE DIVING

In some areas of the world, caverns have formed underwater. These can be explored by divers and, providing that the dives are carefully led, they will be an exhilarating and captivating experience. A flashlight is essential on a dive like this, and all cave dives should be accompanied by a qualified and knowledgeable escort. It is often a good idea to have a guide-line that is fixed outside the cave and can lead you out in emergencies.

EASY PASSAGE
Small caves in the sea can be fun to swim through, but take care you do not get stuck or brush against rocks or stinging animals.

LIFE INSIDE
Caves are usually as teeming with life as any other part of the reef. The creature that has been discovered here is a blue-spotted ray.

IN THE DARK

It is not essential for you to do a night dive so it is best to wait until you are confident or curious enough to want do one. If, at first, you are too nervous the comments of divers as they return from their nocturnal expeditions will no doubt be an incentive for you to join in the next time. Night dives done in cooler water may be a more specialized activity for trained divers.

NIGHT LIFE
You will see that a variety of different creatures appear at night. Many animals come out of the reef to feed. You will also see how some fish actually rest, tucked into the nooks and crannies of the coral.

IN THE LIGHT
You can see only what is in the beam of your flashlight, like this crab.

• SLEEP TIGHT
As fish have no eyelids, when they are sleeping they give the impression that they are still wide awake. If you disturb them, they may be woken up abruptly, so it is best just to illuminate them.

CLOSE RANGE
The possibility of seeing a variety of marine life, like this sea urchin, is greater at night.

—SAFETY FIRST—

AT NIGHT
Dive at a site where natural features make it less likely for you to lose your way. It is wise to select a good shallow site during the day and then leave a shot line there that you can follow down later.

Do not shine your flashlight directly into another diver's face underwater or at the boat on surface as you may blind them. You must make the usual signals with or in the light of the beam

CARE IN CAVES
Diving in confined spaces needs great care. Tie a lead rope securely outside so that you can exit or take a guide. Do not try a cave dive without a full tank of air.

PRECAUTIONS
• Make signals in your flashlight beam or improvise others – such as quick circles with torch meaning OK.
• Be sure you have an experienced guide. Keep closer together than in the day.
• With both dives you must take one powerful flashlight each. Ensure you know how it works and keep it on all the time.

CONSERVATION

Respecting and saving the marine environment.

UNDER THE OCEAN'S SURFACE is a magnificent world of living animals and plants and, as a diver, you are privileged to escape your natural habitat and enjoy the sensations of this vastly different world. Unfortunately, as with all our environment, the ocean has limited resources and steps need to be taken to conserve it. In the early days of sport diving, divers freely pilfered "souvenirs" from the sea bed – shells, corals, and slow-moving animals. It soon became clear that this could not go on without threatening fragile eco-systems and, in some cases, seriously depleting marine species.

RESPONSIBILITY

Throughout the world, conservation organizations exist to encourage and educate all who use the sea, including divers. The majority of the long-term dangers to the oceans are caused by pollution and commercial fishing nets. However, divers have a part to play, especially as particular areas of the shallow sea bed are targeted as dive sites. If these are damaged in any way or destroyed, those who follow us into the sea will not have the opportunity to experience this magical world.

RESPECT RULES
You must observe any notices that are displayed at your chosen dive site. Some of the world's most spectacular underwater locations are being ruined by tourism. Consequently, stringent regulations are now in force.

BUOYANCY
Maintain a level of **buoyancy** that ensures that you do not blunder into the sea bed, or the coral reefs, and thereby destroy delicate organisms which may have taken decades to grow.

SAND CHANNELS
Always follow sand channels when you are swimming through shallow reefs, and try to avoid kicking up or disturbing the sea bed.

MOORING
Prevent your boat from damaging reefs and destroying sea life by anchoring away from the coral or at a designated mooring.

PROTECT & CONSERVE

Help conserve the sea and all its inhabitants for future generations by following these few simple guidelines :
• Join and support those organizations that try to conserve the sea – The Marine Conservation Society, Worldwide Fund for Nature, Greenpeace, and Friends of the Earth, have branches the world over.
• Learn about the marine world – take a marine biology course for divers or a specific marine identification course.
• Don't touch living corals, rest on them, or kick them. Even the slightest contact can cause irreversible damage.
• Do not buy "curios" from the sea. Take photographs, not souvenirs. Souvenirs will only gather dust, but photographs are a personal color record of your experiences.
• Spear fishing is usually forbidden in protected areas – the commercial fishing of modern trawlers has already depleted enough of the fish stocks. If it is legal to collect animals, such as crabs and lobsters, for food, take a limited number and not those that have eggs. Be considerate to local inhabitants – keep clear of fisherman's pots and nets.
• Never drop litter, or leave any waste or pollutants at beaches or dive sites.

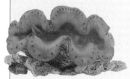

When diving, leave reef animals, such as this blue clam, alone, as they are the "building blocks"of the reef

Don't buy corals, shells, seafans stuffed turtles or souvenirs made of tortoise shell. In doing so you encourage extinction

F*RIEND OR* F*OE?*

Familiarizing yourself with the sea's dangerous inhabitants

W**HEREVER YOU GO UNDER** the sea there is life – darting, swimming, crawling, or even buried in the sand. Areas that are without any life have usually been damaged by humans, pollution and over-fishing can upset the entire eco-system. Before every dive, try to make yourself aware of the indigenous sea life, including any that may be a danger to you. In colder waters, low visibility and temperature are the greatest risks. In warm water, marine life is abundant and there are numerous fish and even some species of coral that you must watch out for. They will not spoil your diving if you are careful. Some of the creatures you should be cautious of are featured here.

IDENTIFYING FISH

Marine animals are far too varied to describe in full, so do acquire a book on the sea life of any area in which you dive. Many guides are written especially for divers. When you are a fully qualified diver, you could even take a course in marine biology. As a rule, try not to touch anything, especially if diving in warm seas.

EELS
Eels have a reputation that is largely undeserved but their teeth can cause a nasty laceration if you provoke them – so don't!

TRIGGER AND URCHIN
Growing up to 70cm (27¹/₂in) long, trigger fish will bite if disturbed guarding their eggs. Watch out for sharp sea urchin spines.

HANDLE WITH CARE

By far the most dangerous animal to be found in the sea is man. Ignorance and foolishness result in more diving accidents than are ever caused by fish. However, there are some creatures of which you should be wary. These are seldom aggressive, but have strong protection, usually in the form of poisonous spines, and if you blunder into them or attempt to handle them, you will probably regret it. Know how to deal with minor stings (see p.21).

CAMOUFLAGED FISH
By wearing a wetsuit and gloves, you will avoid contact with creatures like stone and scorpion fish that may be carefully hidden.

STONE FISH
Stone fish are extremely venomous and should always be avoided as their poison can cause severe pain and sometimes death.

SCORPION FISH
Beware the poisonous spines along the backs of scorpion fish as they will give you a nasty sting if provoked.

ANGLER FISH
Right: The rarer angler fish is best left alone.

SHARKS
Sharks have the most feared reputation of all the ocean creatures and they should always be treated with great respect.

LION FISH
Lion fish drift like harmless, colorful butterflies around coral reefs, but take care as they have toxic spines.

OCEANS OF ADVENTURE

Introducing some of the world's most spectacular dive sites

·

MOST WHO LEARN TO DIVE find that it becomes a passion. Once you are a qualified diver, you will discover the many exciting things for you to do and observe in the world's oceans. To behold the stunning riot of color, unusual shapes, and rare animals is an amazing experience, with every dive offering you something different. It is up to you to do what you wish and, with the ocean covering two-thirds of the world's surface, you will soon find that there is always so much more of the underwater world for you to explore.

1 *Californian kelp forest*

2 *Caribbean sea*

● **CALIFORNIA**
Diving under a canopy of kelp with fish and whales for company is an overwhelming experience.

❷ **THE CARIBBEAN**
The warm seas around the Caribbean islands provide a variety of stunning dive sites set among dramatic coral reefs and wrecks.

❹ THE RED SEA

From shallow, tropical waters, to glorious well-populated coral reefs, the Red Sea provides a perfect location for divers of every standard.

❸ THE MEDITERRANEAN

Throughout this sea, maritime history is evident, with wrecks that can be traced as back as far as 1500BC and those that sank in more recent times.

3 *Mediterranean sea*

4 *Red sea*

❺ SOUTH EAST ASIA

This surge channel through coral in Indonesia provides exciting dives. Such movements of water stimulate sea life and attract larger animals.

5 *South East Asia*

6 *Pacific ocean*

❻ THE GREAT BARRIER REEF

Set off Australia's east coast, the world's largest reef is, for many, the supreme diving experience. This diver is framed by a sea fan.

A SAFE HAVEN

Hugely intelligent creatures, dolphins are greatly loved, but have been exploited by mankind. They are inspiring creatures for us to experience. At the Dolphin Reef at Eilat in the Israeli Red Sea, it is possible for you to have enormous fun diving with them in their natural aquatic environment.

SEAL TREK

In colder waters, particularly at the polar regions, seals are abundant and a diver can sometimes be surrounded by a herd of them. The risks from these mammals are slight, but during their mating season, jealous males have been known to nibble at divers' fins.

DANCING RAYS

With natural agility and grace, rays soar and glide through the water, when not concealed in the sea bed. Riding on the backs of rays and other large aquatic animals is frowned upon by marine scientists, so it must be avoided. Simply to witness or photograph these stunning creatures is a thrill enough.

A GENTLE GIANT

Unlike some other sharks, the whale shark is a slow-moving plankton eater with virtually no teeth. It is the ocean's largest living fish, growing up to lengths of 18m (60ft).

BIG FISH

Species of big fish, such as this potato cod in Australia, can stimulate feelings of fear and apprehension in some people. If treated with consideration, they are relatively harmless.

OFF THE WALL

Diving the great walls or drop-offs on coral reefs can be breathtaking. You can fly over and down a vertical wall, and then along the face, covered with great sponges and fans, while huge free-swimming fish shoal off to sea in the great blue beyond. This famous wall is at Ras Muhammed, in the Red Sea.

GLOSSARY

Words in *italic* are glossary entries.

A

• **A-Clamp** The screw fitting that connects the *regulator* and *pillar valve*.
• **A-Flag** The International Code of Signals flag that means "There is a diver down". It must always be flown by your cover boat and can also be placed on the top of your *SMB*.
• **Artificial Respiration** The emergency method of restarting breathing. It can be performed either by using a mouth-to-nose or mouth-to-mouth method (see pp.21 and 51).
• **Atmospheric Pressure** The force exerted by air at sea level. It is equal to approximately 1 *bar* ($14^{1}/_{2}$ lb/in^2).

B

• **Bar** The unit of measurement that indicates the pressure of air. 1 bar is equivalent to *atmospheric pressure* or $14^{1}/_{2}$lb/in^2. The term bar has largely supplanted the term atmosphere as the measurement of pressure. The units are largely interchangeable: 1 bar is equal to 0.986 atmospheres.
• **Bezel** The adjustable ring on a watch or a compass. It is set to indicate an initial time or position.
• **Buoy** See *Surface Marker Buoy*.

Diving with a surface marker buoy is essential in currents; it allows your cover boat to keep an eye on your exact position as you dive

The A-Flag warns of your presence

• **Buoyancy** See *neutral buoyancy*.
• **Buoyancy Compensator (BC)** A jacket that can be inflated and deflated with air from your *scuba* tank. It is sometimes called a "stab jacket".
• **Burst Lung** Pressure damage that is caused by *compressed air* expanding in the lungs on ascent, due to the diver holding their breath. It can be avoided in an emergency by sharing an air supply with a co-diver or by performing a *free ascent*.

C

• **Compressed air** Air that is taken from the atmosphere and compressed to high pressure (usually around 200 *bar*/3000lb/in^2) for use in *scuba* tanks.

D

• **Decompression Sickness (DCS)** A diving disorder caused by bubbles of nitrogen forming in the bloodstream. The condition is sometimes referred to as "the bends" (see pp.52-53).
• **Decompression Stop** A pause close to the surface at the end of a dive to allow the elimination of any excess nitrogen and therefore prevent *DCS*.
• **Decompression Tables** Specially calibrated tables that allow divers to calculate safe depths, times, and rates of ascent during their dives, thus helping to avoid *decompression sickness*.
• **Direct Feed** The tube that connects the tank to the *BC*, enabling it to be inflated with *compressed air*.
• **Dump Valve** A valve on your *BC* that rapidly releases air, thus halting an uncontrolled ascent.

E

• **Ear clearing** This is also known as equalizing, and it is the technique of opening your eustachian tube, while you are descending, so that you can balance the pressure inside your ear. An absolutely essential process for all who dive, it is usually easily achieved by simply holding your nose and blowing gently against the pressure.

F

• **First-stage** The part of your *regulator* that attaches to your tank. It reduces the pressure of air that is fed to the *second-stage*.

• **Free Ascent** An emergency method of going back to the surface. It involves the diver breathing out all the way up.

L

• **Log book** A journal that sets out each of your dives in detail, both as a personal and qualifying record.

M

• **Mask Squeeze** A condition caused when pressure inside your mask drops. The pressure can be balanced by blowing out through your nose.

N

• **Neoprene** The sponge-like artificial material that is used to manufacture wetsuits and other diving accessories.

• **Neutral buoyancy** The state where a diver neither floats or sinks, but maintains an optimum position in midwater. Negative buoyancy means that you have an inclination to sink, while positive buoyancy means that you have a tendency to float.

• **Nitrogen Narcosis** Intoxication at depth caused by excess nitrogen. It can cause problems if the symptoms are not recognized (see pp.56-57).

O

• **Octopus Rig** A spare mouthpiece that attaches to your regulator for use by a companion in an emergency.

• **O-Ring** The washer that is set in the *pillar valve*. It forms an airtight seal for the regulator.

P

• **Pillar valve** The valve that is set into the top of your tank, allowing the release of *compressed air*.

• **Pre-dive check** A thorough check on all equipment with your co-diver. It includes all quick-releases and connections, that you are switched on, and have your mask and fins ready.

• **Purge valve** The diaphragm at the front of the *second-stage* of the *regulator*. Applying pressure to it provides extra air and expels any drops of excess water that may have entered into the regulator mouthpiece.

R

• **Recompression chamber** The apparatus that recompresses a diver who is suffering from either *burst lung* or *decompression sickness*. It recompresses a diver and then decompresses them back to *atmospheric pressure*.

• **Regulator** The part of your *scuba* which automatically reduces air pressure to that of surrounding water, providing air as needed. It consists of a *first-stage* that fixes to the air tank, and the *second-stage*, which is held in the diver's mouth. It can also be referred to as the demand valve.

S

• **Scuba** Meaning self-contained underwater breathing apparatus, this equipment allows divers to breathe underwater. It works by adjusting the air that the diver breathes to match the pressure of the surrounding water.

• **Second-stage** The part of the *regulator* including your mouthpiece, the *purge valve*, and the exhaust valve.

• **Shot line** A vertical line that extends between a surface buoy and sea bed, and fixes a position.

• **Surface Marker Buoy (SMB)** A buoy that attaches to a diver marking their position. It is essential when drift diving or diving in a current.

*The **BC** is a vital piece of diving equipment that allows you to control your **buoyancy** underwater*

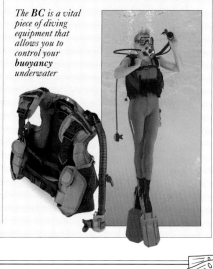

INDEX

A

air 17
  in the body 19
  filling tanks 76
  pressure 16
  sharing 40-1
air tanks 15
  entering the water 33
  filling 76
  suiting up 30-1
  tank boots 15
  testing 76
air valves, clearing 30
angler fish 87
artificial respiration 21, 51
ascents 37
  boat diving 67
  controlled 44
  decompression 52-3
  ditch and retrieve 48
  dump valve 45
  free 48, 55
  recovery 50
  sharing air 41
  shoreline diving 61
  surface marker buoys 71

B

backward rolls 39, 64-5
bags 77
barrel rolls 39
"the bends" 18, 52-3
boat diving 13, 62-71
boots 10
breathing
  deep diving 57
  ditch and retrieve 48
  during descents 38
  resuscitation 51
  sharing air 40-1
  snorkeling 27, 45
buoyancy, snorkeling 26, 28
buoyancy compensator (BC) 13
  ascents 44
  controls 43
  deep diving 57
  descents 36
  ditch and retrieve 46-9
  dump valves 45
  entering the water 32

maintaining buoyancy 42
maintenance 77
  quick-releases 46
  recovery 50-1
  sharing air 41
  shoreline diving 60
  suiting up 30-1
  tropical dives 66
buoys, surface marker 13, 70-1
burst lung 17, 38

C

California 88
cameras 81
Caribbean 88
casualties, recovery 50-1
cave diving 82-3
clearing:
  air valves 30
  ears 33, 37, 60
  masks 34, 49
  snorkels 27
co-divers:
  emergencies 54-5
  nitrogen narcosis 57
  pre-dive checks 31, 63, 75
  recovery 50-1
  sharing air 40-1
cod 91
color, underwater 17
coming up see ascents
communication 22-3
compasses 12, 79
compressed air see air
compressors 76
computers 78
conservation 84-5
consoles 12
coral reefs, conservation 84-5

D

decompression 52-3
decompression sickness (DCS) 52-3, 57
decompression stops 53, 57
decompression tables 53
deep diving 56-7
demand valves 14

depth gauges 12, 78
descents 36-7
  breathing during 38
  shoreline diving 60
  surface marker buoys 70-1
distress signals 51
ditch and retrieve 46-9
dives:
  surface dives 29
  tropical dives 66-7
dolphins 90
dry suits 11
dump valves 45

E

ears:
  air in 19
  clearing 33, 37, 60
eels 86
Eilat 80, 90
emergencies 50-1, 54-7
entering water 32-5
  backward rolls 64-5
  boat diving 62-5
  forward rolls 63
  shoreline diving 59
equipment 10-15
  instruments 78-9
  maintenance 76-7

F

fear 54-5, 57
fins 8, 10
  ascents 44, 45
  ditch and retrieve 47
  shoreline diving 59
  snorkeling 26
first aid 20-1
fish 83, 86-7
fishing 85
fitness 18-19
flags, signal 13
flashlights 12
  signals 23, 83
forward rolls 38, 63
free ascents 48, 55

G

gauges 78
  checking 58, 67
gloves 10
going down see descents

Great Barrier Reef 89

H
hand signals 22-3

I
inflatable dinghies 64
instructors 8-9
instruments 78-9

J
jump entries:
    boat diving 62
    snorkeling 28

K
knives 12, 58
    signals using 23

L
ladders 69
language 22-3
legs:
    ascents 44
    rolls 38-9
light and color 17
lion fish 87
log books 74
    boat diving 67, 69
long john 11
lungs:
    air in 19
    burst 17, 38

M
magazines 81
maintenance of equipment 76-7
marker buoys 70-1
masks 10
    boat diving 62, 64
    clearing 34, 49
    distorted vision 29
    ditch and retrieve 47, 49
    entering water 32
    jump entries 28
    misting up 32
    pressure effects 38
    snorkeling 26
medical emergencies 20-1
medical examinations 19
Mediterranean 89
mouth-to-mouth resusitation 21
mouth-to-nose resuscitation 51
mouthpieces 14

ditch and retrieve 47, 48
    removal 35
    sharing air 40-1

N
narcosis 54, 56-7
natural buoyancy 44
navigation 79
neoprene:
    boots 10
    gloves 10
    maintenance 77
    wetsuits 11
neutral buoyancy 42, 66
night diving 57, 83
nitrogen 17, 52-3
nitrogen narcosis 54, 56-7

O
O-ring seal 15, 30
octopus rig 15, 41
oxygen 17

P
panic 54-5, 57
photography 80, 81
physics 16-17
pillar valves 15
pre-dive checks 63, 75
pressure, physical laws 16
pressure tubes 15
purge valves 14-15, 41

Q
quick-releases 46

R
Ras Muhammed 91
rays 90
recompression chambers 53
recovery 50-1
recovery position 21
Red Sea 80, 89-91
regulator 14
    maintenance 77
    retrieval 35
resuscitation 21, 51
retrieving equipment 48-9
rolling 38-9

S
safety 9
    basic rules 75
    cave diving 83
    first aid 20-1
    fish 86-7

night diving 83
scorpion fish 87
sea urchins 86
seals 90
sharing air 40-1
sharks 87, 91
shops 76
shoreline diving 58-61
shot lines 56
signals:
    flags, 13
    flashlights 23
    hand 22-3, 51
snorkeling 26-9, 45
snorkels 10
South East Asia 89
stings 20, 87
stomach, air in 19
stone fish 87
surface dives 29
surface marker buoy (SMB) 13, 70-1
surfacing techniques 44-5
    see also ascents
swimming ability 18

T
tanks see air tanks
trigger fish 86
tropical dives 66-7

V
videos 80, 81

W
walls 91
watches 12, 78
water pressure 16
weight belts 12, 26
    descents 28
    getting into small boats 68
wetsuits 8, 11
    care of 77
    snorkeling 26

GETTING IN TOUCH

PADI
1251 East Dyer Road
Suite 100, Santa Ana,
California 92705-5605
Tel: (714) 540-7234

PADI
Unit 9, 306 Estate
Broomhill Road
Bristol BR4 5RG, England
Tel: (0272) 711717

ACKNOWLEDGMENTS

Reg Vallintine and Dorling Kindersley would like to thank the following
for their valuable help and expertise in the production of this book:

Thanks to Brian Pitkin and his assistant Derek Biginton for the pool and
location photography. Philip Gatward and his assistant Dean Belcher for studio
photography. Kieran Sykes and Mark Stanton for modelling. Scubapro for the
generous loan of their equipment, also London Diving Centre Ltd and Ocean
Leisure Ltd. The Janet Adegoke Leisure Centre for the use of the diving pit.
Red Sea Sports Club Hotel, and Ed's Photo Shop for the loan of gear and
developing the location photography. Sam Grimmer for design assistance,
Kieran Sykes for proof reading, Hilary Bird for the index, Dr. John Betts for
medical advice. Janos Marffy for all line and full colour illustrations,
John Plumer (Cartographic Department) for the map on pp.88-89.

The following for additional photography: Paul Springett, Israel p.81 (tm), p.83
(tr, tm, ml, mr, bl), p.86 (bl, br), p.87 (mr,bl). E. V. Green p.81 (mr), p.87 (ml).
Ardea: Valerie Taylor p.89 (cr), David Nance p.53 (cl), p.89 (tr), Val Taylor p.91
(t), p.91 (cl). Bruce Coleman Ltd: John Murray p.90 (bl), p.91 (b). Planet Earth:
Kurt Amsler p.88 (bl), Gary Bell p.89 (bl), John Lythgoe p.89 (tl), Doug Perrine
p.87 (br). Seaphot Ltd: David Rootes p.90 (cr), Norbert Wu p.88 (cl).

Author's note: We all had a lot of fun doing the underwater photography in
the Red Sea, helped by Roni Klein of the Red Sea Sports Club, and the dolphins
of Dolphin Reef. Our photographer worked tirelessly to get the best shots, and
even my editor Sarah Larter, designer Emma Boys, and series editor Jo Weeks
took the plunge and became divers. Why don't you follow their example?

Many thanks to Divers World who
arranged our shoot at the Red Sea
Sports Club, which is a BSAC school
& PADI five-star centre based in
Eilat. Contact Divers World to
arrange your learn-to-dive holiday.

Divers World,
IHS Travel Limited
26 Temple Fortune Parade
London NW11, England
Tel: 081 905 5252
Fax: 081 458 3234